AN OUTLINE OF ANGLICAN MORAL THEOLOGY

by

LINDSAY DEWAR

LONDON
A. R. MOWBRAY & CO LTD

© A. R. Mowbray & Co. Ltd. 1968

Printed in Great Britain by
Alden & Mowbray Ltd at the Alden Press, Oxford

SBN 264 65561 3

First published in 1968

AMICO MEO
CYRILLO EDUARDO HUDSON
PRESBYTERO
THEOLOGIAE MORALIS ANGLICANAE PRAECEPTORI
DEFUNCTO ADHUC LOQUENTI

Contents

Introduction   *page* vii

1. THE ANGLICAN APPROACH TO MORAL   1
   THEOLOGY

2. HUMAN CONDUCT   21

3. CONSCIENCE   43

4. CASUISTRY AND MODERN PROBLEMS   65

5. SIN AND IMPERFECTION   108

6. PUNISHMENT AND FORGIVENESS   128

7. THE CHRISTIAN STANDARD AND IDEAL   147

8. THE NATURE OF ANGLICAN AUTHORITY   173

9. THE MORAL THEOLOGIAN IN A POST-   198
   CHRISTIAN SOCIETY

   Additional Note on the Authority of Convocation   215

   Index   217

ACKNOWLEDGMENTS

The thanks of the author and publishers are due to the following for permission to quote extracts:

The Central Board of Finance of the Church of England, *Ought Suicide to be a Crime?*; The Church Assembly Board for Social Responsibility, *The Church and the Atom* and *Sterilisation: An Ethical Enquiry*; The Clarendon Press, *Karl Marx's Capital* by A. D. Lindsay; Constable Publishers, *The True Wilderness* by H. A. Williams; Darton, Longman & Todd Ltd., *Clinical Theology* by Frank Lake; Eyre & Spottiswoode (Publishers) Ltd., *Citizen and Churchman* by William Temple; Faber & Faber Ltd., *The Sanctity of Human Life and the Criminal Law* by Glanville Williams; Hodder & Stoughton Ltd., *Church and State in England* by C. F. Garbett; Longmans, Green & Co. Ltd., *Conscience and its Problems* by K. E. Kirk; Macmillan & Co. Ltd., *Christus Veritas* by William Temple and *The Faith of a Moralist* by A. E. Taylor; Oxford University Press, *Textbook of Psychiatry* by D. K. Henderson and R. D. Gillespie; Penguin Books Ltd., *The Physical Basis of Personality* by V. H. Mottram; University Tutorial Press Ltd., *A Manual of Ethics* by J. S. Mackenzie.

Should any acknowledgment have been omitted inadvertently, then this oversight will be rectified in subsequent editions if brought to the attention of either the author or the publishers.

Introduction

THE PURPOSE of this book is twofold. First, as the title
suggests, it is intended to provide an outline of Anglican,
as contrasted with Roman Catholic, moral theology. As
is well known, there are numerous text books of Roman
moral theology, but there is no Anglican text book. The
reason for this is, partly at least, that Anglican theology
generally is less systematic and authoritarian than Roman,
although the latter is rapidly changing before our eyes.
Consequently Anglican moral teaching is less systematic and authoritarian and more difficult to reduce to
the form of a text book. On many moral questions there
is no single Anglican position, as there is in the Roman
Catholic Church. To take a conspicuous example, in the
matter of the legitimacy of the use of contraceptives, there
is no authoritative Anglican ruling to compare with the
Roman Catholic teaching on this subject. Other similar
examples could be quoted, and that is why it is much
harder to write an Anglican than a Roman text book of
moral theology. On the other hand, it makes it less necessary to have an Anglican text book on the subject, because
so much more is left to the judgement of the individual
conscience. Yet, if the latter is to make a satisfactory
judgement, it must be provided with the material with
which to form that judgement; and it is the duty of the
Anglican moral theologian to provide that material.
One of the main purposes of this book is to do just this.

The example which we have taken, we may note in passing, shows clearly the advantages of the Anglican approach. The Roman Catholic may have an authoritative rule in this matter, as in many others, but the rule may chafe his conscience. Thus it is an open secret that the Roman Catholic ruling about the illegitimacy of the use of contraceptives is not only challenged but widely ignored by many of the faithful today. 'The bed is shorter than that a man can stretch himself on it; and the covering narrower than that he can wrap himself in it' (Isaiah 28.20). If the Anglican conscience has less detailed guidance, at any rate it has more room to breathe freely. Anglican moral theology, therefore, is more easily accommodated in an 'Outline' than in a text book. Perhaps the time will never come when an Anglican text book of moral theology can be adequately written. At all events that time has not come yet.

The second main purpose of this book is to assist two classes of people: (*a*) the clergy, who have the delicate and important task of giving moral guidance both formally in church and informally outside it; and (*b*) the ordinary Anglican lay man or woman called to face perplexing moral problems. As readers of this book will discover, the leading Anglican moralists have always thought it essential that souls should not be 'spoon fed' in ethical matters, but rather taught how to feed themselves on solid and nourishing diet. I venture to hope that this book supplies it.

I have tried to write compendiously, rather than diffusely, as the manner of too many is, and in such a way as to interest the average reader who may have no technical knowledge in this field but is looking for guidance 'in each perplexing path of life'.

I thank my friend, Mrs. W. J. Cook, for most kindly typing the whole MS. I wish also to thank Canon W. E. Purcell and Canon G. B. Bentley for reading through the typescript and for making various helpful suggestions for its improvement; but they are not responsible for what I have written.

Quotations from the Bible are taken from the Revised Version (1884) unless it is otherwise stated.

L.D.

I

The Anglican Approach to
Moral Theology

IT IS almost a hundred years since a committee of the
clergy of the Church of England was formed 'for the
construction of a *Manual of Moral Theology* suited to
the growing needs of the English priesthood'. As a result
there appeared in 1882 the volume by the Rev. James
Skinner entitled *A Synopsis of Moral and Ascetical Theology*.
This book, which the author did not live to see through
the press, is a learned survey of the field which he
thought such a book should cover, together with an
exhaustive list of authorities which would have to be
consulted. In the Preface to this book—which is hard to
come by since most of the copies printed were destroyed
by fire—Mr. Skinner wrote: 'Whether a Manual of
Moral Theology for the use of Priests in the English
Church shall ever be compiled remains to be seen. But if
it is ever to be undertaken, it must, in the largest sense,
include Spiritual or Mystical Theology. . . . The whole end
of our *Manual* must be practical not speculative; and
therefore the wide field of Ascetical Theology must be
open to us, from which to draw for the building up of
souls.' He went on: 'I am in harmony with the convic-
tions of the best spiritual guides of the Western Church
when I say that one of the best qualifications of a good
Confessor is to be neither systematic, nor personal, nor

absolute in his principles of direction. "Systems" are mischievous in politics, in philosophy, in education, in economy. The spirit of mere system is a danger everywhere; in the domain of conscience it is an absolute evil. Of course there are great principles of moral and spiritual direction which never change, to which also there is in each conscience a responsive chord by which it touches God. But these principles co-exist with an endless variety of forms in which they are applicable to individuals. . . . The initiative of healthy direction does not come from the Confessor, still less does it come from a type which has been formalised into an ideal. It comes straight from the penitent, enlightened by the gift of God the Holy Ghost, as to his special need. The mission of the Priest (this is Fénelon's view) is to aid, to perfect, to complete. He is to take for his basis that of which the individual soul is capable; not that which he puts there, but that which he finds.'[1]

The project in the mind of Skinner and the fellow members of that committee was never taken any further. Even if it had been, it would by this time have become out of date. But in the emphasis on the importance of linking Ascetical and Moral Theology it is quite in line with the best thinking today. It is the more surprising that Skinner's synopsis of the field takes relatively little account of the work done by Jeremy Taylor and Sanderson, although, of course, their names appear in the lists of authorities quoted. Moreover, Skinner took a step backwards rather than a step forwards in thinking of spiritual direction far too exclusively in terms of the confessional—a mistake which the great Carolines did not make. This mistake of Skinner was largely repeated by those who sought to foster the study of moral theology in the Church of England in the last century. This is intelligible enough in view of the great increase in the

[1] James Skinner: *A Synopsis of Moral and Ascetical Theology* (1882).

number of those members of that Church who made use of sacramental confession, but it was, all the same, unfortunate. For it is of the greatest importance to appreciate the fact that the place of moral theology in the life and thinking of the Church is quite distinct from the place of the confessional. Even if the latter were, *per impossibile*, to disappear entirely, the need for moral theology would remain, since it is nothing less than the detailed study of Christian conduct in the light of its theological basis and background.

In view of what has just been said, it would seem that the best starting point from which the moral theologian in the Church of England today can proceed is to be found in the principles laid down by Sanderson and Taylor. Although unfortunately these two men, who were contemporaries, worked independently, their general standpoint is similar, and they are both true representatives of the genius of Anglicanism. The principles to which they adhered are far more closely allied to the thinking of the present day than are the principles of scholasticism which have governed Roman Catholic moral theology.

The first question at issue here is the nature and meaning of repentance. The doctrine of repentance can only too easily be taken to be a licence to sin. This was too often the result of Roman Catholic moral theology. If we are led to believe that we can deliberately lead a selfish and a worldly life, and that all will be well at the end if we repent, we are—so the Carolines maintained—being gravely misled. The Christian Doctrine of repentance is safe only when it is coupled with the command 'Be ye perfect'. Jeremy Taylor is very careful to explain what is meant by this command. It is perfection of intention and of endeavour—not of achievement. 'The state of regeneration is perfection all the way, even when it is imperfect in its degrees. The whole state of a Christian's life is a state of perfection. Sincerity is the formality or the soul of it: a hearty, constant endeavour is the body or material part of it; and the mercies of God accepting it in Christ, and assisting and promoting it by his Spirit of grace, is the third part of its constitution, it is the Spirit.'[1]

This carries with it an interesting corollary, commonly expressed by the popular phrase 'back seats in heaven'. Taylor expresses the matter thus: 'Although God exacts not an impossible law under eternal and insufferable pains, yet he imposes great holiness in unlimited and indefinite measures, with a design to give excellent proportions of reward answerable to the greatness of our endeavour. Hell is not the end of them that fail in the greatest measures of perfection; but great degrees of heaven shall be their portion who do all that they can always, and offend in the fewest instances. For as our duty is not limited, so neither are the degrees of glory: and if there were not this latitude of duty, neither could there be any difference in glory; neither could it be possible for all men to hope for heaven, but now all may: the meanest of God's servants shall go thither; and yet there are greater measures for the best and most excellent services.'[2]

Thus is laid down the first principle of Anglican moral theology. It is that the Christian life must be lived in all sincerity. Taylor truly says: 'Not that lukewarmness is by name forbidden by any of the laws of the Gospel, but that it is against the analogy and design of it.'[3] There is no question of forgiveness being a kind of dodge or charm to bring us to heaven. Our aim must be perfection and nothing less. At the same time all men are not equally *capax Dei*. We can only do our best with the talents entrusted to us. 'For if the readiness is there, it is

[1] *Unum Necessarium*, Chap. 1, § 4.   [2] *Ibid.*, Chap. 1, § 2.
[3] *Ibid.*, Chap. 4, § 4.

acceptable according as a man hath, and not according to that he hath not' (2 Cor. 8.12). Taylor himself here inclined too far in the rigorist direction; but the general principle which he set forth stands, and is a complete safeguard against the abuses and charges which have been levelled against the Christian doctrine of forgiveness in general and the practice of confession in particular. Thus we refute the insinuation that moral theology is a 'set of rules for the breaking of rules'.

Closely allied with the foregoing is the attitude of the Carolines towards the distinction between mortal and venial sin. This distinction was basic to scholastic moral theology and was developed by Aquinas and fully authorised by the Council of Trent. According to this teaching sins can be estimated according as they do or do not imply aversion from God, who is man's Last End. So Aquinas argues. If a sin involves aversion from God, it is mortal. If it does not—for example, when it is committed through infirmity or lack of knowledge—it is only venial. He illustrates this by a physical analogy. If the physical body declines completely from the principle of life, it will die and there is no remedy. But if it only partly declines from the principle of life it continues to live and may be restored to health. Again, in matters of thought, if the basic principles of truth are removed, the position is hopeless; but if these principles remain although the argument is faulty, the error can be put right.

This approach to sin was abhorrent to the Carolines. Yet they do not dispute, as some Christian moralists, or would-be moralists, have done that sins differ in degree. Thus Taylor refers to our Lord's saying to Pilate that he was guilty of a lesser sin than those who had handed him over (S. John 19.11). But he denies that this means that sins can be classified into mortal and venial. He argues that the difference between big sins and lesser sins is due to the fact that in the case of the former we have in fact the conjunction of two or three different sins, 'entangled like the twinings of combining serpents' (*op. cit.*, Ch. 3 §2). Thus, for example, adultery is worse than fornication because it is a combination of impurity and injustice, and to steal money from a church is worse than ordinary theft, because it is dishonesty plus sacrilege. Consequently, he maintains that sins 'differ only in nature, not in morality; just as a greater number or a greater weight: so that, in effect, all sins are differenced by complication only, that is, either of the external or the internal instances'.[1]

There is undoubtedly some truth in what Taylor says here. Some sins are, so to say, compound sins and therefore more serious. But this does not prove that all single (*i.e.* not compound) sins are of equal gravity, and it is flying in the face of reason to assert that because all sin—even the most trifling—is undesirable and against God's will, it follows that such sins cut us off from God as do the graver sins. It is surely mistaken to the point of absurdity to say with Taylor: 'It is a less evil that all mankind should be destroyed, than that God should be displeased in the least instance that is imaginable.'[2] Nevertheless, the Caroline moralists were right in pointing to the danger inherent in any hard and fast distinction between mortal and venial sin. Unless this danger is fully recognised and steps are taken to guard against it, we shall end up with a morality that is less than fully Christian. It was, and still is, a weakness of the traditional strain in moral theology, that frequently the dangers have been ignored and the generosity of the Christian ethic has tended too often to degenerate into

> 'the lore
> of nicely calculated less or more.'

[1] *Unum. Necessarium*, Chap. 4, § 4.   [2] *Ibid.*, Chap. 3, § 3.

This is a question to which we shall have to return in a later chapter.

A third way in which the Carolines, and Taylor in particular, blazed a new trail was in their endeavour to show that moral theology is detachable from the confessional and not entirely dependent upon it. This comes out clearly in the Preface to *Ductor Dubitantium*. Taylor writes there: 'For I intend to offer to the world a general instrument of moral theology, by the rules and measures of which, the guides of souls may determine the particulars that shall be brought before them; and those who love to inquire, may also find their duty so described, that unless their duty be complicated with laws, and civil customs, and secular interests, men that are wise may guide themselves in all their proportions of conscience: but if their case be indeed involved, they need the conduct of a spiritual guide, to untie the intrigue, and state the question, and apply the respective rules to the several parts of it.'

This is an important statement. Taylor does not deny the need for a spiritual guide, but, on the contrary, goes on to emphasise what is said here by adding 'Men will for ever need a living guide'. It is perhaps significant however, that he does not suggest that such guidance and direction need necessarily be given in confession. Furthermore, he makes it clear that he holds that in general his aim is to make every man his own casuist; and he goes on to say that this aim is much more likely to be realised if preachers will 'preach and exhort to simplicity and love; for the want of these is the great multiplyer of cases. Men do not serve God with honesty and heartiness, and they do not love him greatly; but stand upon terms with him, and study how much is lawful, how far they may go, and which is their utmost step of lawful, being afraid to do more for God and for their souls than is simply and indispensably necessary. ... But the good man

B

understands the things of God; not only because God's Spirit, by secret immissions of light, does properly instruct him; but because he hath a way of determining his cases of conscience which will never fail him.'

In the foregoing the Carolines sowed seeds which have been long germinating.

It is clear that Taylor and the other Carolines were feeling their way towards a new conception of moral theology, entirely free from a legalistic basis. As we have noticed, they moved away from the position which Aquinas laid down, but without making a complete break. Unfortunately, however, they did not pin-point the basic weakness in his position, which has seldom been perceived. This, I suggest, is that he failed to grasp the implications of the fundamental difference between the Eternal Law and human law; and they did the same. Yet Hooker had pointed the way, when he said that: 'The being of God is a kind of law unto his working; for that perfection which God is, giveth perfection to that which he doth.'[1] In other words, the eternal law of God is nothing but the manifestation[2] in time and space of the nature and being of God. So Hooker says again: 'They err, therefore, who think that of the will of God to do this there is no reason beside his will.'[3] But he does not follow his own pointer when he simply says that oftentimes we cannot tell the reason, without explicitly adding that this reason is in the nature of God's eternal Being. Thus eternal law is immutable as is God Himself, 'with whom is no variableness nor shadow of turning'.

As against this, human law is both mutable and subject to error. Aquinas fails to describe the situation accurately when he argues that what the first principles and axioms of speculative reason are to the sciences, so is

[1] *Laws of Ecclesiastical Polity*, 1.2.
[2] In Aquinas this manifestation is called the Natural Law. *S.T.* Ia IIae Q.91, a.2.
[3] *Laws of Ecclesiastical Polity*, 1.2.

the eternal law to human laws. Unfortunately the latter are not so securely founded, and they are fundamentally different in their nature, too often reflecting not the goodness and changelessness of God (like the first principles of reason) but the sinfulness and mutability of men. That is why we can never be really satisfied with a moral theology based on law; unless we make it perfectly clear that we are thinking of law in the first sense as reflecting the perfect Being of God and not the frailty and mutability of man. In fact, the cardinal weakness of the Thomist moral theology is that Aquinas turned his back on the distinction which the Greeks had firmly grasped between nature (φύσις) and law (νόμος), the former immutable, the latter arbitrary and subject to change. Consequently a moral theology based on law was always likely to surrender to the weaknesses of legalism; and this, as everybody knows, is what has happened, and we are still under its influence. The time is rapidly approaching, however, when Anglican moral theology will finally find its true nature, which was adumbrated, but unfortunately not clearly discerned, by Jeremy Taylor and his contemporaries in the seventeenth century.

We proceed, then, to consider some of the recent protests of Anglican writers against the traditional moral theology. These may be summarised, I think, under two broad headings. In the first place, we have those writers who wish to jettison the whole conception of law in morality and to substitute for it Christian Love. This, they argue, is the sum and substance of it all. 'Love, and do what you will.'[1] We should at the outset notice here a point of great importance to which Canon Waddams has recently drawn attention. He rightly says: 'In one sense it is true that the only absolute standard in the New

---

[1] I have pointed out elsewhere that Augustine did not use his dictum in this way, *Moral Theology in the Modern World* (1964), pp. 51 and 52.

Testament is *Agape*, but it is not the subjective *Agape* of the individual, but the *Agape* of God which alone sets the standard for all men.'[1] He proceeds to point out that this objective *Agape* is in fact a shorthand description of the Nature of God to us-ward and includes the whole order of creation. Consequently, moral laws are subsumed in that *Agape* even as the colours of the spectrum are subsumed in white light. Therefore the New Testament can say 'God is *agape*', but this is by no means the same as saying '*Agape* is God'. To argue thus—and many would-be Christian moralists do argue thus—is to commit a logical howler. If the error, already mentioned, whereby 'law' was identified with erring and arbitrary human law, had not established itself so strongly, we should not have been so blind as to the true relationship between *Agape* and law.

Another aspect of this species of protest against the traditional moral theology is represented by the argument that New Testament morality is intensely personal whereas law is essentially impersonal. Once again, we see the domination of the conception of human law. This is *per se* impersonal, distributing, or attempting to distribute, justice with strict impartiality. But the eternal law is not impersonal in that sense. It is true that it does not contravene justice, but it transcends it. It is, indeed, intensely personal, even to the numbering of the hairs of our head. God does not create by mass production; there are no crowds before him. Yet it does not follow that Christian morality is solely concerned with individuals and not with society and social institutions. 'The Kingdom of God' is a theme which is basic in the New Testament. We do less than justice to the concept of *agape* if we ignore this. The truth underlying this protest is that in the New Testament the whole life of the Christian is overshadowed by the thought of the *agape* of

[1] H. Waddams: *A New Introduction to Moral Theology* (1964), p. 80.

God revealed in the Incarnate Son of God, and is a response to that revelation, made in the power of the indwelling Spirit, who dwells not only in each baptised individual but also in the *Koinonia* of the Body. Thus there is 'a law of Christ' (Gal. 6.2), though it is very different from any human law. But we simply misrepresent the situation if we suppose that this means that the Christian need not keep any rules of morality. For the believer there are certain moral qualities or fruits which he is expected to manifest, and for the average person, at least, this means giving heed to such rules as shall commend themselves to the mind of the *Koinonia*. They are still rules, even though they are generically different from human rules and regulations. The latter are a manifestation of imperfect and erring human minds and wills. These are the manifestation of the mind of the Spirit. There is a close parallel here to the relation which exists between civil law and canon law. Civil law proceeds from the mind of the Sovereign authority in the State and exists in statutes and sundry regulations. Canon law is rooted in the customs of God's people, who are under the divine guidance of the Holy Spirit. William Temple rightly said that one of the greatest misfortunes which ever befell the Christian Church was when canon law became assimilated to civil law. These two proceed from entirely different sources even as do Eternal Law which is of God and human law, which is of men.

The second type of protest against the traditional approach to moral theology is based on the position that it does not pay sufficient attention to empirical data, but follows the 'high priori road' too exclusively. There is considerable force in this contention, although it is worth pointing out, in passing, that the modern type of Christian moralist who would base everything on 'Love' is every bit as much *a priori*. We must, therefore, now

examine with care the position of those who urge the
need, in this modern scientific and experimental age,
for more empiricism in our moral theology.

In a recent book,[1] I pointed out in this connexion that
it is a serious mistake to expect to be able to establish
moral standards by empirical methods alone. The most
that we can hope to achieve by the experimental method
in this field is the establishing of factual evidence, but the
evaluation of these facts cannot be achieved experi-
mentally. I also pointed out that it is important to remember that the experimental method can be followed
only in community. Thus modern experimental science
is a community product, the result of the corporate
efforts of a multitude of scientists whom no man can
number. So must it be in the field of moral theology. And
this is now being made very clear to us in a new way by
the remarkable development of what is known as Clinical
Theology, under the leadership of Dr. Frank Lake. For a
generation or more there has been a small body of Christians
who have been trying to work out the implications for
Christian theology and practice of Freudian psychology—
for that is basically what Clinical Theology is doing—but
they have been voices crying in the wilderness. But in the
past six or seven years the Church at last is beginning to
wake up to the importance of these issues for the understanding of her task. In particular, this is being manifested
in the criticism that the traditional moral theology of the
Church will have to be rewritten, or, at least, greatly
modified. On this account we must, therefore, proceed to
enquire how far this is the case.

In the past, as we have already noticed, moral theology
has been based on law. It has been understood as the
application of the law of God in relation to human
conduct, and this, I, for one, believe that it still is, always
provided that 'law' is here rightly understood as being

[1] *Moral Theology in the Modern World*, p. 34.

the manifestation of the character of God, as revealed in the New Testament, to us-ward. It is, however, in the human aspect of the subject that the findings of Clinical Theology have drawn our attention in a new way to the importance of the empirical approach. In particular have these findings thrown light upon the significance of the Christian Community—the Koinonia of the Spirit, in New Testament language—in adopting the empirical approach to the solution of our moral problems.

These moral problems, with which moral theology is concerned, are essentially problems of living together,[1] for the simple reason that man is a social being. When he enters the world and begins to live an independent life, he is intimately dependent upon his mother. The importance of the new studies here is that it is now possible to understand in detail the psychological development of the new-born child. This is assisted in some cases by the use of certain drugs[2] which enable a person to relive the first two years of his life in memory. We now know that, for the first year or two of life, although materially he is separate from his mother, he is not psychologically separate. He is in 'the womb of the spirit' only gradually becoming psychologically independent, until the crucial moment comes when he first thinks of himself as an independent being and uses the word 'I'. Even then he is still dependent upon his mother, who has to perform a task of great delicacy in giving him just the right degree of support—not too much and not too little. It is during this crucial period in his life that the child forms what is called its disposition or basic psychological attitude to life.

[1] *Cf.* Butler: 'That mankind is a community, that we all stand in a relation to each other, that there is a public end and interest of society which each particular is obliged to promote, is the sum of morals.' Sermon IX upon *Forgiveness of Injuries.*

[2] Notably LSD 25 (lysergic acid); but it seems likely that the dangers and drawbacks in the use of this drug will progressively lead to its disuse. There is an analogy here to the disuse, or virtual disuse, of hypnosis in psychiatry.

In the days before the Freudian psychology, we had no real understanding of the nature of our dispositions, nor of the way in which they were formed, because we had no knowledge of the unconscious mind or of the psychological mechanism of repression. It was the genius of Freud to bring to light the significance of this, which has revolutionised the study of human nature. We are now able to understand how the basic faulty dispositions are formed, and to appreciate in detail the various resulting difficulties which we all have in solving the problem of life, which is the problem of living together.

According to moral theology, this problem is triangular. We have to be rightly adjusted not only to ourselves and to our fellow men, but also to God. Freud attached an atheistic theology to his psychology; but it is now generally recognised that there is no necessary connexion between the two. In fact, what we know of Freud's own early life as a Jew, as a member of a despised race, enables us to see why it was that he was not able to 'see straight' in matters of religion. Yet Freud shows no awareness of the effect of these early influences in fashioning his materialistic philosophy, which does not necessarily follow from his psychology. If he had done so, this part of his teaching might have been entirely different. The moral theologian today, nevertheless, ignores the positive and psychological aspects of Freud's teaching at his peril. Nor, as an Anglican theologian, is there any reason why he should wish to do so; for this new knowledge reinforces some of the elements in the traditional Anglican approach to this subject.

In the course of this book, we shall come across the various basic types of maladjusted, *i.e.* not co-operative, dispositions, as they are now understood in Clinical Theology, in their bearing on moral theology. Here, however, we must draw attention to the fact that Clinical Theology has emphasised the importance of the Caroline endeavour to show that moral theology must not be too closely associated with the confessional, as it has been in Roman Catholic practice. As soon as Freud put forward his new teachings, it was perceived that psycho-analysis had some similarity to the practice of sacramental confession. There is at least a superficial parallel between the priest and the penitent and the analyst or psychiatrist and the patient. It was, however, soon pointed out that the analogy could be dangerously misleading inasmuch as the penitent could, *ex hypothesi*, confess only sins of which he was conscious, whereas the analyst was concerned rather with unconscious material. Nevertheless, the analogy is not without its bearing on the work of the priest in dealing with sinners; for in his work as confessor he is called upon to give spiritual direction, and in order to do this efficiently he must understand the character of the penitent. It is, however, not possible to do this without a good knowledge of the mind's workings and particularly the operations of the unconscious mind. More than that, it is clearly desirable, if he is not to give advice which may do more harm than good, that he should have some knowledge of the unconscious mind of the particular penitent with whom he is dealing. But how is he to get this in the confessional? Usually there is no time for this, for such knowledge can be gained only if there is ample time. Apart from this difficulty, the priest–penitent relationship, where the former sits as judge, is not at all the same as the psychotherapist–patient relationship, where the former is in no sense judge. Indeed, that is the one role which he must not play.

It would seem, therefore, that there is a strong case for arguing that it is desirable, at any rate in many cases, to separate the office of the director from that of the confessor. The confessional is the place where we receive 'the benefit of absolution'. Detailed 'Spiritual counsel and advice' is better given outside it. This does, however, raise the problem of the 'seal' in a new form. Could it be extended to cover the spiritual directions of the director, if he is the same person as the confessor? This is a practical question to which an answer must be found, and found as soon as possible.

There is another way in which the empirical approach to moral theology is being illuminated by clinical theology and this also harks back to the typically Anglican approach, as it is found (for example) in Skinner. It will be remembered that in the passage already quoted from his *Synopsis* he said: 'The initiative of healthy direction does not come from the Confessor, still less does it come from a type which has been formalised into an ideal. It comes straight from the penitent, enlightened by the gift of God the Holy Ghost, as to his special need.' The truth of this statement has been abundantly shown by the practice of modern psychotherapy, and it means that moral theology should be centred not on any system or set of rules but upon individual persons. In other words, it must in this sense of the term be empirical. Souls cannot be standardised, although it is true that our clinical theology has shown most clearly that they can be classified. Yet it remains true that each of us is an individual, himself or herself, and nobody else in the world. There can be no doubt that the modern reaction against the traditional moral theology of law derives much of its force from this conviction.

In this connexion I venture to quote what I have written elsewhere: 'The course of any analysis, or prolonged psychiatric treatment, cannot be mapped out in advance, even by the most experienced psychiatrist. To quote from a modern exponent of the art: "A wind begins to blow—softly, and, at the start, almost imperceptibly; but (and this is the point) where it listeth. The *direction* of the new current within the man's life is not fixed in advance." The patient has, in one way or another, become cut off from the instinctual roots of his being—in a word, from the beneficent leadings of the Holy Spirit, the Life-Giver. Healing comes when the Holy Spirit is allowed by the patient to have free course within him. The task of the analyst is to assist the patient to allow this to happen—not *de haut en bas* (that leads to deadlock) but by coming alongside his patient and sharing, so far as may be, his experience with him. There is only one word which can do justice to this attitude and that is the word *agape*; and it is precisely this which is the most distinctive "fruit" of the Spirit, according to the New Testament. It is the work of the Paraclete. The Paraclete—literally one called alongside to help—here takes on a new meaning: for this is an exact description of the good psychiatrist of whatever school.'[1] Here we have the authentic language of clinical theology. The pastor is frequently referred to as the paraclete. Above everything else he is taught to be an understanding listener, and he must learn the therapeutic value of the right kind of listening and of taking case histories. Indeed, it may be hoped that one of the major results of the work of clinical theology—although it may be some time before this particular result is achieved—is that the general image of the clergyman may be changed, so that first and foremost he may be thought of as an understanding person. At present this is far from being the case. More often he is regarded as one ready to condemn; and so the average lay person is apt, albeit often unconsciously, to adopt a defensive attitude in his dealings with the clergy, and certainly the last person to whom many of them would turn for advice and spiritual help is the parson. It is impossible to exaggerate the harmful effects of this state of affairs. Could this image

[1] *The Holy Spirit and Modern Thought* (1959), p. 177.

be changed, the change would do more for the work of evangelism than all the other forces of evangelism put together. The clergyman should be 'an interpreter, one among a thousand' (Job 33.23).

There is a further illustration of the empirical aspect of moral theology which is provided by clinical theology. It springs from group psychotherapy. In the first instance this seems to have come into being chiefly owing to the fact that there are not enough psychiatrists to go round; so that it is literally impossible, especially in mental hospitals, to give much individual treatment. Consequently psychiatrists have been compelled to get their patients together in groups for treatment. For some types of mental illness, group therapy has been found most successful; and when clinical theology got going by bringing together groups each of a dozen young priests for instruction, the advantages of the group became especially evident. This, indeed, is what might have been expected; for, according to the New Testament, the Church is a brotherhood, in which the Holy Spirit is the bond of unity, creating 'the fellowship (*koinonia*) of the Spirit'. Christianity is not 'what a person does with his solitariness' nor 'the flight of the alone to the Alone' but is centred upon the *ekklesia*, the company of those who have been 'called out' by God into the new life in Christ. They are bound together by *agape*, which however it is to be translated or described, is certainly a community word. Nor must it be forgotten that we are taught to worship one God in Trinity and Trinity in Unity.

All this must be reflected in our moral theology. It can be claimed that in the past these insights have not been open to the moral theologian. He knew of course that Christianity is not a private affair between the soul and God and that there is a social dimension of all our duties as Christians, even the most private and personal. 'There is no word so secret that shall go for nought'.[1] But there was a tendency among those who compiled treatises on moral theology to present the Christian life as the individual pursuit of certain aims and virtues, comprised in a system of virtues, without adequately taking into account the actual situation of the individual Christian. Indeed, until the coming of Freud this was impossible, since the unconscious aspect of the mind and its growth was a sealed book. We now see that the corporate empirical aspect of spiritual direction is of primary importance, and that it is possible for the moral theologian to take this into account. Indeed, it is essential. In the past, there have always been spiritual directors who have excelled by reason of outstanding gifts of intuition which have enabled them to discern the hidden problems of the soul. But these have always been the exception. Furthermore, such gifts and knowledge could not be transmitted; nor does any systematic attempt seem to have been made even to try to pass on to young clergymen the spiritual wisdom by which these confessors were enlightened.

Thus clinical theology is showing us the great importance for spiritual direction of the corporate aspect of the life of the Christian. The precise significance of this can be discovered only empirically. It does not follow from this that there are no immutable moral principles, as some mistakenly suppose, but it cannot be denied that the way in which they are to be applied must be 'seen' by each individual for himself. Moreover, we are learning now that this may most easily be brought to pass in many cases—or even be possible at all—when he or she is a member of a small group or 'cell' in the Body of Christ. Thus it is becoming clear that spiritual direction can come through membership of a group or cell in the Body of Christ.

[1] Wisdom I. II (A.V.)

Of course, there is nothing new in the idea of illumination coming through small groups of Christians meeting together. The Society of Friends and the Methodist class meetings are sufficient to show that. But what is new is that clinical theology is enabling us to understand as never before the reasons why such groups so easily develop in the wrong way; and there is a good deal more which we have to learn about this. A modern writer has said: 'We must learn a great deal about the dynamics of groups and study why some are successful and some are not. Those which are successful are those which have broken through to real acceptance and spontaneous love and they are rare. More often than not, the apparent success of a small group is achieved because the people involved in the group are all nice middle-class people—articulate, well bred, living in respectable houses to which the group can go without fuss or embarrassment—but they are often unaware of the people who couldn't be contained in such a milieu. Very often a small group is 'successful' because in the most respectable way it has scapegoated all undesirable members and formed itself into a tight little collusive huddle. Groups can become either too academic or too chattily superficial as ways of avoiding personal involvement.'

We must, therefore, not underestimate the difficulties which confront the members of such a group. The danger of pietism is very great, as also is the danger of steering clear of personal involvement. At the same time it is true—and from our reading of the New Testament we should expect it to be true—that the mutual acceptance which membership of such a group implies leads to a deeper understanding of the fellowship of the Spirit (*Koinonia*) than can be obtained in any other way, and, in many cases, to a deeper self-knowledge also.

2

Human Conduct

MORAL THEOLOGY is concerned with human actions. It presupposes that for some, at least, of his actions every normal human being is responsible. Those for which he is not responsible are of two kinds: (*a*) those which are not freely performed, and (*b*) those which are done in ignorance. Both of these conditions require most careful consideration.

In the first place, every act for which a person can be held responsible must be performed freely. This raises the difficult question as to what exactly is meant by 'freely'. We may notice, at the outset, an attempt to evade this issue by arguing that this simply means freedom from external restraint, and that it is not inconsistent with a strictly deterministic view of human conduct, according to which human conduct is, in theory, strictly predictable, like all other events. The only reason why we cannot thus predict it, it is argued, is that we do not have access to a full knowledge of all the data. Nevertheless, it is said, it is reasonable to hold a person responsible for his actions, since his conduct can be influenced by corrective procedures. 'Personal responsibility means that an individual is liable to corrective procedures when his actions violate the limits imposed upon behaviour by society. The criminal is liable to imprisonment and restraining; the psychotic is liable to medical treatment. The subjective concepts of "will power to do differently" or "self-control" are irrelevant to this concept of personal responsibilty.'[1] Surely this argument puts the cart before the horse. We do not hold a person responsible for his actions because his conduct can be changed by the infliction of punishment upon him. We inflict punishment upon him because we hold him responsible for the actions on account of which he receives punishment. Thus the restraint which we impose on the criminal who is sent to prison is of a different order from the restraint which we impose on the insane person who is shut up in a mental hospital. Dr. Boe, in the passage which we have just quoted, refutes himself when he places the criminal and the psychotic in the same category. It is impossible to hold to a strict doctrine of determinism and at the same time hold to belief in human responsibility.

We must pass on, therefore, to consider the question of freedom and determinism. Oceans of ink have been poured out on this question, but a great deal of the argumentation has been beside the point and would never have taken place if two important considerations had always been borne in mind. The first of these is that the issue should not be set between what are called Determinism and Indeterminism or Libertarianism. This leads off the discussion on the wrong foot and dooms it to failure; for it deals with the better known in terms of the lesser known, and in those terms tries to explain the former by the latter, the personal world in terms of the impersonal. It presupposes that we understand what is meant by 'causation' in the material world and that we can then apply this knowledge to explain human conduct. Here again we are guilty of a *hysteron proteron*. We do not really understand at all what is meant by saying that in the material world an event is determined by preceding events. All we can rightly say about this is

[1] E. E. Boe, 'Personal Responsibility: A Psychologist's View', in *The Medico-Legal Journal*, Vol. xxxiv, Part I.

that we observe invariable sequences of events, like being followed by like in orderly fashion; but the connexion between the events is not observed and cannot really be explained. Plato pointed this out long ago in the *Phaedo*.[1] On the other hand, in dealing with human conduct we have immediate insight which enables us to understand what we mean by the power of choosing between different courses of action. We also are quite familiar with the difference between performing an action deliberately and performing the same action 'against our will'. In a word, we know the meaning of 'willing', and that this is *per se* free.

This, however, does not involve the concept of 'uncaused' actions. That irrelevant concept has bedevilled the whole controversy and is the result of beginning this discussion at the wrong end, as we have said.

The second consideration which must be remembered when we are discussing the question of freedom and responsibility is the harmfulness of what McDougall called 'the inveterate tendency to reify' in dealing with the problems of psychology. When we talk about 'ideas' or 'feelings' or 'emotions' we can easily be deceived into thinking that we are concerned with distinct entities similar to material bodies. In fact, we are concerned with nothing of the kind. We are dealing with the stream of consciousness, which is mental and not material, and therefore is strictly indivisible. In the present context it is the term 'motive' which is the mischief maker. There is no such thing as 'a motive', or 'an incentive' which can be the 'cause' of a human action. If we use these terms we must always remember that we are using them to describe what is happening when a human being is performing a single and indivisible action. If we forget this, it is fatally easy to discuss the question as if the action was 'caused' by the preceding 'motives' and to argue that,

[1] Plato: *Phaedo*, 98.

C

therefore, the agent was not free, since the act was the result of the interplay of the preceding motives and that the strongest motive or motives won the day. Such a statement as this is, in fact, entirely meaningless, because it is quite impossible to attach any meaning to the phrase 'the strongest motive'. When two different weights are placed in a pair of scales, it makes sense to say that the scale which holds the heavier weight will always sink, because it is possible to check independently which is the heavier of the two weights. But there is no way of checking which is the stronger of two 'motives'. Consequently to say that the stronger of two motives always wins simply means that the motive that always wins always wins, which does not throw much light on the question. Such absurd arguments as these would never have confused this controversy, if the disputants had always remembered that 'motives' are not entities.

We claim, therefore, that everybody knows from his own experience what is meant by free choice, since we all exercise it every day. It is a power limited in various ways by our circumstances, but it is a veridical phenomenon known to us all. It was this fact of experience to which Dr. Johnson bluntly referred when he said: 'We *know* our will is free and *there's* an end on't'.[1] If we hold fast to this approach to the question of freedom we are enabled to assess the right relationship of freedom to compulsion. There are undoubtedly circumstances when a person feels compelled to perform a certain action without his freedom being overridden. On the contrary, he feels never more free. Thus it is with all acts of inspiration. The artist, the poet, the musician all testify to this experience. They are impelled to produce their works of art, and it is significant that in such circumstances we use the word 'impelled' rather than 'compelled'. They can do

[1] Boswell's *Life of Johnson*, Vol. 2, p. 601 (L. F. Powell's revision of S. B. Hill's edition).

no other, and yet at the same time they choose to do it. There is in this experience no contradiction. That is why it is so misleading to contrast freedom and necessity, and, we have argued, this would never have been the case if the discussion had not too often started at the wrong end. Thus it is that the Christian recognises that his freedom is not restricted but enhanced by his experience of the grace of God 'whose service is perfect freedom'. His freedom is not like the mechanical freedom of the weathercock able to face in any direction with equal facility. That would be slavery to every passing influence. The free man is not 'capable of anything'; that is far from being a complimentary epithet. In the last resort, as S. Augustine saw, freedom is freedom to do what is right and good.

Such, then, is freedom as understood and postulated by the moral theologian. But he is not out of the wood yet. He has to face another kind of objection, and that is the effect of unconscious influences. It may be argued that he feels that he is making a free choice, when he performs a particular action, whereas in fact he is doing it under the influence of unconscious forces. This position is based on the evidence of post-hypnotic suggestion. The patient, under hypnosis, is (for example) told that on waking up he will at once blow his nose. This he does, but on being asked why he will give some other reason, because he is not able to recall the suggestion given under hypnosis. All that this evidence proves, however, is that undeniably unconscious influences come into play when we are making acts of conscious choice. It does not prove that all acts of conscious choice are solely the result of such influences. What it does prove is that unconscious influences are among those factors which limit and restrict the power of human choice. There is, indeed, positive evidence to show that unconscious influences do not always over-ride the power of choice and render it completely illusory. It is known that when the hypnotist makes suggestions which are in conflict with the moral principles of the patient they are not carried out. There is, for example, a case on record of a girl hypnotised in front of a class of medical students who was told, under hypnosis, that when she woke up she would immediately strip naked. Instead of doing this, she quietly walked out of the room! There is also evidence to show that those who carry out post-hypnotic suggestions, although they do not recall the suggestions, do not feel that they are carrying out deliberately willed actions.

There is yet one other line of attack against freedom which the moral theologian has to face, and that is the attack made in the name of physiology. Whatever we may think when we make an act of choice, so runs the argument, it is illusory because all our thoughts and feelings are governed by what is happening in our nervous system. Not only choice, but also consciousness itself, is therefore illusory, or, at any rate, mind and matter are two aspects of the same thing. Here we are once again involved in putting the cart before the horse. We know mind and consciousness and choice immediately. We know physiology, like any other science, inferentially. It is mistaken to suppose that we can explain the former in terms of the latter. As a modern physiologist has said: 'I know, for instance, that "I am" much more certainly than I know that the pen with which I am writing these words "is". I know of the existence of the pen only through the sense impressions I obtain from it. But I need no sensory approaches to tell me that I am. The truth of my own existence is much more immediate to me than the truth of the existence of my pen. The one I get directly, the other I have to obtain through sensory endings in my skin, muscles and joints, or through my eyes, and a complex mechanism of nerve fibres and brain cells of different hierarchies.'[1] Whatever some may say, an act of human choice is *not* identical with physical changes in the nervous system, and to say that it is 'caused' by them is not really intelligible; for we have not explained what is meant by 'caused' in this context.

The moral theologian, therefore, holds that freedom is an undeniable fact of human experience, but that this in no way implies that a free man or a free woman, in exercising an act of choice, is 'capable of doing anything' just as a weathercock, if well oiled, is equally capable of pointing in any direction. We are free to act within limits. These limits are partially constituted by our characters, the sort of persons we are. George Washington could not tell a lie; probably the Archbishop of Canterbury cannot get drunk. We are also limited by the fact that we are all subject to various impulses and inhibitions, many of which stem from the sphere of the unconscious over which we have no conscious control. But this does not alter the fact that in the case of the normal individual there always exists the power of exercising an act of deliberate choice.

The existence of the aforementioned impulses and inhibitions and their effect on human freedom and responsibility has been clearly recognised recently by English Law in the Homicide Act of 1957 in the concept of 'diminished responsibility'. According to this, 'Where a person kills or is a party to the killing of another, he shall not be convicted of murder if he was suffering from such abnormality of mind (whether arising from a condition of arrested or retarded development of mind or any inherent causes or induced by disease or injury) as substantially impaired his mental responsibility for his acts and omissions in doing or being a party to the killing'.[2] This provision differs in a most important

---

[1] V. H. Mottram: *The Physical Basis of Personality* (Pelican Books).
[2] *Op. cit.*, Part 1, Clause 2, § 1.

respect from the famous McNaghten Rules which previously governed the law in this matter. For the latter held that a person must be held responsible for his actions unless either he did not know what he was doing or did not know that it was wrong, thus making responsibility rest only upon adequate knowledge. The Homicide Act, on the other hand, makes it clear that responsibility also depends upon emotional factors which may be outside a person's control. In other words, it recognises that both knowledge and freedom underlie responsible action. In certain pathological states the area of freedom may be so greatly restricted as to reduce the responsibility of the agent to a minimum—sometimes perhaps to vanishing point.

Obviously this new concept of diminished responsibility is a dangerous one and capable of being misused. It is certainly much more difficult to apply than the old McNaghten rules; but, in theory at least, it makes it possible to make a more accurate assessment of the responsibility of an individual for his act or acts. As such, the moral theologian need have no quarrel with it.

We shall have to return shortly to a discussion of the several constituents of the human act, but first let us pass on to consider the other requirement for responsible action, viz. knowledge. It is universally agreed that, if the agent is to be held accountable for what he does, he must know what he is doing. For example, a person would not be held responsible for anything which he did while walking in his sleep. As Aristotle said, we give praise or blame only to voluntary action, and this means not done under compulsion or through ignorance (E.N. 1110 b).

This raises the important question: What kind of ignorance? For when we begin to consider the matter with care we recognise that sometimes ignorance does not excuse. It is a maxim of civil law that *Ignorantia legis non excusat.* Otherwise it would be an easy way out for any dishonest person to say concerning any illegal offence which he had committed that he did not know that it was illegal. The moral theologian, however, is in a different position from the lawyer inasmuch as he must assume that he is dealing with people who are morally sincere. Consequently he has to say that sometimes ignorance of the law does excuse a person from blame. For example, a person who had never heard the name of Christ could not be blamed for not knowing that it is wrong to retaliate against those who have injured us. Similarly a person in a foreign country and ignorant of the language which he had had no opportunity to learn, could not be blamed for not being able to read a public notice. Such ignorance is said by the moral theologian to be invincible, and it is essential, from his point of view, that he should be able, in a given case, to decide whether the agent's ignorance is or is not of this kind.

Thus we are led to the vital distinction between two kinds of ignorance, viz. vincible and invincible. The former is culpable ignorance; the latter is inculpable, and it is described by Aquinas as *ignorantia quae studio non superari potest* (*Summa Theologica,* Ia IIae Q.76, a.2). On the other hand, ignorance which could have been dispelled by the agent is called vincible, and this, the moral theologian teaches, is culpable if it relates to matters which he might have been reasonably expected to know, but not otherwise. Is it possible to state in general terms what these matters are?

First, there are some things which every normal person may be assumed to know—*aptus natus est scire* (*ibid.,* Q.76, a.2): for example, the difference between right and wrong. This is often questioned, especially today, when the whole conception of natural law is being frowned upon. Nevertheless, as Kirk said, 'We may not appeal to "the natural law": but we do appeal to "the conscience of society", and expect everyone who is possessed of the use of his reason to be aware of the dictates of that conscience. There are few communities in which, for example, outrageous and inhuman brutality would be condoned on the excuse that no one had told the offender not to do it. We may quarrel with the scholastic mode of statement if we wish, and no doubt it led to much erroneous and dogmatic tabulation of the content of "the natural law" and so impeded the free development of thought and institutions. But in one form or another the conception is an anchor and safeguard of corporate life; and as such every community recognises it in fact, though it may not accept it as a philosophical postulate by name.'[1]

Secondly, in every trade or profession there is a certain amount of knowledge relevant to the trade or profession which a person may be reasonably assumed to possess. For example, a physician could not plead that he did not know that the medicine given to the patient was poisonous, or the lawyer that he was ignorant of a crucial point of law. In general, as Sanderson says, the individual may reasonably be expected to use that diligence in acquiring knowledge which the importance of the case requires and which men of prudence always observe in their own important affairs.

Nevertheless, if we press for a precise meaning to be attached to the word *studium* in the definition of Aquinas, we do undoubtedly run into difficulties. Is it possible, for example, to employ this conception of invincible ignorance to cover the case of a person who remains an unbeliever, even after he has had a clear exposition of the Faith put before him? It surely is a misuse of the word 'ignorance' to call such an individual invincibly ignorant. Could S. Thomas have been reasonably called invincibly ignorant when he said that he would not believe until he

[1] K. E. Kirk: *Ignorance, Faith and Conformity* (1924), pp. 36 and 37.

had put his fingers into the print of the nails? It may well be true that the unbeliever, in the sight of God, may have excuse for his unbelief, when all the circumstances of his life are taken into account, but surely the excuse should not be brought under the heading of invincible ignorance so that his ultimate salvation may be presumed. There is, indeed, a really fatal objection to this use of the conception of invincible ignorance, and it is this. Salvation consists in the true knowledge of God as he is, 'in knowledge of whom standeth our eternal life' (*quem nosse vivere*). It is, therefore, surely a contradiction to say that a person can be saved without having this saving knowledge. Jeremy Taylor seems to be on the right lines when he says: 'I am not here to dispute what is likely to be the condition of the heathen in the other world: it concerns not us, it is not a case of conscience: but we are sure that all men have the law of God written in their hearts; that God is so manifested in the creatures, and so communicates himself to mankind in benefits and blessings that no man has just cause to say that he knows not God. . . . But it is very certain that without a man's own fault no man shall eternally perish: and therefore it is also certain that every man that will use what diligence he can and ought in his circumstances, he shall know all that in his circumstances is necessary. . . . Every man hath enough of knowledge to make him good if he please: and it is infinitely culpable and criminal, that men, by their industry, shall become so wise in the affairs of the world, and so ignorant in that which is their eternal interest.'[1] He sums up the matter as follows: 'Therefore by moral diligence is to be understood, such a diligence in acquiring notices, as can (1) consist with our other affairs, and the requisites of our calling and necessities; (2) such as is usual by ourselves in the obtaining things which we value; (3) such which is allowed by wise men, such

---

[1] *Ductor Dubitantium*, Book IV, Chap. i, Rule 5.

which a spiritual guide will approve; (4) and such as we ourselves do perceive to be the effects of a real desire.'[1]

Perhaps this is as far as we can go in attempting a precise definition of what is meant by 'culpable ignorance'. In a given instance it is often difficult to say how far a person is 'innocently ignorant', to use Jeremy Taylor's expression. This, however, does not really affect the great value and importance of this distinction for moral theology. The important point is that the moral theologian can clearly recognise, as the lawyer cannot, that there *are* occasions when ignorance of the moral law is not culpable.

We have now to consider the constituents of the human act, and we are immediately faced by some differences of terminology, which have caused a good deal of confusion. There are several different words in common use to denote the several 'parts' of a human action: viz. motive, intention, purpose, end, circumstances and consequences. It is important to the moral theologian to be quite clear as to the meaning of these various terms. He must also bear in mind the caution mentioned above not to forget that these words do not denote specific entities but are merely attempts to distinguish different aspects of something which is, in strictness, one and indivisible. It is, however, convenient and useful to make use of such terms in seeking to understand the nature and morality of human actions, provided that their meaning is clearly defined. Unfortunately this is not always the case, and different writers use these terms in different senses, and this has caused and still causes much confusion.

Let us begin with the two words, motive and intention. There has been a good deal of confusion in the way in which these words are used. Some moralists have used them as if they were identical in meaning. Thus, for

[1] *Ibid.*

example, Jeremy Taylor uses them interchangeably. In *Holy Living* one of his three instruments of a holy life is what he calls 'purity of intention' to do all for the glory of God. But the context shows that by 'intention' here he means 'motive' and this he does regularly in his *Ductor Dubitantium*. Sanderson does the same thing, although he draws a distinction (which is sometimes useful) between the inward act of intending and the objective intention. This identification of motive and intention is most confusing; for in fact they are quite different. For example, my intention at this moment is to write these words as part of a book on moral theology. There is no question about that. But what are my motives? They might be vainglory, or desire to make money, or to spread the knowledge of moral theology. Whatever they may be, they are clearly quite different from the intention. The motives of an action provide the driving power of the action and constitute the 'reason' why it is performed. In most actions there is only a single intention—or at the most a double intention; whereas there are probably few, if any actions, prompted by a single motive. Nearly all acts are the result of several motives, varying both in strength and moral quality. Motives as we say are often 'mixed', and whereas the intention of an act is conscious in the case of every deliberate action, motives are often partly unconscious. This custom of failing to distinguish between motive and intention, therefore, is not conducive to clear thinking. The intention of an act is constituted and indicated by the nature of the act itself and is obvious to all. The motives are the driving power behind the act and are not open to inspection. They may be deeply hidden even from the agent himself.

What has just been said about motive and intention is borne out by common usage. Take, for example, the saying that the road to hell is paved with good intentions.

This could not possibly be taken to mean that the road to hell is paved with good motives. We all recognise that good motives are praiseworthy and valuable, even if they are not enough of themselves to constitute a good action. But mere good intentions are valueless unless they issue in the appropriate action. When the priest turns to the communicants and says to them: 'Ye that do truly and earnestly repent you of your sins, and intend to lead a new life' he is not speaking to them about their motives but about their prospective behaviour. When the girl's father asks the prospective suitor what his intentions are regarding his daughter, he is not enquiring about his motives. The intention of an action describes the nature of the action not the reason why it is performed. That is the motive. If I take a revolver out of my pocket and point it at my neighbour and pull the trigger my intention is plain enough; but not my motive. It may take a long trial in order to elucidate that.

It should be clear from what has been said that for an action to be wholly good both the motive, or motives, and the action itself should be good. Some acts are in their nature good—for example, telling the truth, generous giving and so forth. But if I tell the truth to my neighbour because I wish to hurt his feelings or to humiliate him, this action is vitiated by a bad motive. A bad motive will mar any action, whereas a good motive alone is not enough to constitute a good action. This is clear from the meaning commonly attached to the remark to the effect that a person 'means well'. This indicates that his motives may be good, but that his actions are not always the same. Much evil has been done by men with good motives. A person with good motives may act harmfully and irresponsibly.

Something further must be added about the variety of motives. It has just been said that most acts derive from more than one motive. These several motives may differ

in moral value. Some may be impeccable, but others
may not. In such cases, the act results from mixed
motives. Moreover, some of the motives of an act may be
unconscious and entirely hidden from the agent. Does it
not follow, therefore, that we can never be sure that all
the motives behind an action are good, and, in consequence, that we can never confidently say of any act that
it is wholly good, inasmuch as shady motives may be
lurking in the background? The answer to this difficulty
is to say that when several motives lie behind an action,
some of these motives are dominant. Provided that the
dominant motives are good, we need not worry ourselves
about the rest. For example, if a person gives money to
Oxfam moved by a desire to help the starving, but is glad
when he sees his name on a subscription list subsequently
published, clearly he has been motivated not only by
compassion but also by vanity. But if he did not know
that his name was going to be published and never gave
the matter a thought it is clear that his dominant or
ruling motive was compassion and not pride. In consequence, the goodness of the action is not destroyed by
the presence in the background of less exalted motives.
In assessing our motives in performing any action,
therefore, it is enough to make sure that our dominating
motives are good. We do not have to search with a
candle to see if less worthy motives are hidden away.
That is the path to scrupulous pride not to genuine
virtue.

   In contrast to the motive, the intention is the purpose
to perform this or that specific action. It is characteristic
of human beings that their actions are purposive. That
is to say they come into existence not simply because of
what has happened in the past, but because of something
which is, as we say, 'purposed' to happen in the future. It
is this intention or purpose which leads to the performance of all deliberately performed human actions.

Human action is purposive. The behaviourist indeed denies this, but in so doing he is contradicting the first-hand experience of taking action which we all have. In doing this we believe that what we are doing is caused by something in the future, not by something in the past. We wish to bring something to pass or to prevent something from coming to pass. To deny this is to deny what no unsophisticated person can possibly doubt. If the experience is illusory, nobody has succeeded in providing a convincing explanation of how the illusion originated.

Having distinguished between motive and intention, we now turn to consider the circumstances of an action. Here it is necessary to remind ourselves again that the distinctions which we are making are the result of dissecting something which, in strictness, is not divisible. To some extent the circumstances of an action are part of the action. An act performed in no circumstances at all would be unthinkable. Some writers speak of motive as being among the circumstances in which an action is performed. This, however, is not altogether satisfactory, since the motives of an action are so intimately associated with it. Perhaps the best way of dealing with this question is to distinguish between inseparable circumstances and separable circumstances. The former are such circumstances as go to constitute the action. Thus murder is killing a person in certain circumstances, viz. when it is done deliberately and with personal malice. Similarly, adultery is sexual intercourse with the wife or husband of another person. These circumstances respectively constitute the act and make it what it is.

On the other hand, there are what we have called separable circumstances which may accompany any action, but which need not do so and which are variable. Such circumstances will clearly affect the moral quality of the action. Some of these are called mitigating circumstances, and these lessen the gravity of the offence. Thus theft of food committed by a starving man is less culpable than if committed by one who is well fed; indeed, it might be totally excusable, if the man were desperate. Drunkenness on the part of one who had been encouraged from childhood to drink is more excusable than it is in a normal individual. Contrariwise circumstances may increase the evil of an action. Thus to steal from a church is worse than to steal from a private house, for sacrilege is added to the guilt of theft. To kill your father is worse than to kill a stranger. To seduce a virgin is worse than to consort with a prostitute, and so forth.

It is commonly agreed by moralists that certain actions are neither good nor bad, but morally indifferent in themselves. For instance, it is morally indifferent for a woman to wear a red hat or a blue hat, ignoring (as we may) aesthetic considerations; it is morally indifferent whether I drink tea or coffee for breakfast. But circumstances may give such actions moral status. If, for example, the woman wore the red hat rather than the blue one, in order to annoy, or specially to please, her husband, that would change the character of the action. If I take tea instead of coffee in order to spare my hostess trouble, the character of the action is altered. Consequently it is clear that the separable circumstances in which an act is performed may determine the moral quality of the action. For a woman to appear in the nude before a strange man would generally be condemned as an act of indecency; but if the man were a doctor about to examine her the situation would be completely changed. Some might say the same if she were an artist's model provided that strict safeguards were observed.

Thus it is clear that separable circumstances may determine the morality of an action, so that they may have to be taken into account in passing judgement on it. They may turn a morally indifferent act into one which may be either blameworthy or praiseworthy. They may turn an action which is good in itself into a bad action; if, for example, a nurse were to go to sleep while on night duty. But can they turn an act which is *per se* bad into a good one? This raises the question as to whether any action is wrong in itself. It is argued by some that in fact there is no such thing as an action which is *per se* wrong, since every action which we normally regard as wrong is so described because it is an act performed in certain circumstances. For example, fornication is sexual intercourse performed in certain circumstances which are condemned; but, it is argued, sexual intercourse as an act is morally indifferent. The same applies to killing. Murder is wrong because it is killing in circumstances which are condemned; but killing is not *per se* wrong— e.g. in war[1] or in judicial executions. Nor, it is argued, is lying *per se* wrong. It is only wrong in those circumstances in which failure to tell the truth is condemned. This argument is rather artificial. It is really a question of definition. We can, if we like, deny that there are any universal moral laws forbidding lying and murder and sexual immorality, and try to deal with each individual case separately. On the other hand, we can postulate general moral laws which make certain classes of actions *per se* wrong, and then take into account extenuating circumstances which may apply to particular cases. In this case, it is clear that certain actions can be described as *per se* wrong. If we take the other view, we are still forced back to certain moral principles which must be regarded as basic and which ultimately determine the morality of our actions; and in the last resort these principles must indicate whether an action is right or wrong. This is, therefore, largely a dispute about words.

So we still have to face the question whether circumstances can turn an action which normally is admittedly

---

[1] Pacifists would of course deny this.

wrong into one which is right? The answer which the
moral theologian must give to this is, No. If, for example,
fornication is wrong, it cannot be made right—as in the
notorious instance—because when a young man slept
with a particular girl he was able to prove his virility
and regain his confidence. This is to do evil that good
may come, and to assert that the end justifies the means.

This brings us to the last of the constituent factors in
human action which we have to consider, viz. the
consequences. Just as the circumstances of an action
are closely bound up with it and in many cases are
inseparable from it, so it is with the consequences. It is
convenient here to make a threefold distinction between
the attendant consequences, the immediate consequences
and the remote consequences of an act. The attendant
consequences are really part of the action. For example,
if I drink a glass of beer I thereby experience certain
attendant consequences, viz. the taste and the smell of the
beer, the after sensation of drinking, the sight of the
dwindling amount of liquid in the glass and so forth. If
these experiences were abstracted from the action, there
would be nothing left to constitute the action. Further,
these are closely connected with what may be called the
immediate consequences of the action, viz. the quenching
of my thirst, and the feeling of satisfaction which follows
at once upon the drinking of a glass of beer. But if beer
does not agree with me, the consequences will be different.
If, again, I have been brought up as a strict teetotaller,
and this is my first glass of beer, the consequences will
again be different. Whatever the circumstances in which
an act is committed, however, there will always be both
the attendant consequences (closely allied to the circumstances yet distinguishable from them) and the immediate consequences, which will have to be taken into
account by the moral theologian, even if it is not always
easy to draw a clear line of demarcation between them.

D

There are also the remote consequences which he may have to consider. But first of all let us consider the immediate consequences of an act. How do these affect the morality of the act? We have already considered one case in which an attempt was made to justify an act of fornication on the ground that the immediate consequences were good, and we have said that the moralist must condemn this judgement. Otherwise the door would be open wide to immoral conduct. Nevertheless, this argument is often put forward. For example, when the first atomic bombs were dropped on Hiroshima and Nagasaki many defended the acts on the ground that, although they killed and disabled many thousands of non-combatants, including women and children, they brought the war to a sudden end, which was a good thing. Another example is provided by the newly devised practice whereby organs are transplanted from the bodies of the dead to assist the living. If this practice is to be validated, it is not enough simply to argue (as so many do) that the consequences are good. Other factors must be taken into account. Otherwise we are saying that it may be sometimes right to do evil that good may come and that the end justifies the means. No moral theologian will admit this.

There are, however, cases where a single act leads to two immediate but distinct consequences, one good and one bad. In such cases, moral theologians have widely agreed that it is legitimate to perform the action for the sake of the good consequences and to ignore the bad. The stock instance is that of the girl who jumps out of the window in order to avoid being raped. The good consequence of this act is that she preserves her virginity, and this is her object in performing it. If in fact she kills herself in the process, this evil consequence was not directly willed and so does not invalidate the action. This is known as the principle of the double effect. It must be carefully distinguished from the case in which a bad act is performed to ensure good consequences. This is the case of *a single act* which involves two *inseparable* but distinct consequences, one good and one bad, and only the former is directly willed. To take another instance, the oft-quoted case where the surgeon must choose between saving the life of the child or the mother. Whatever he does, or refrains from doing, either the mother or the child is likely to die. He is thus forced into a position of causing something bad to happen. If he operates, the infant will die; if he refrains from operating, the mother will die. He has to choose, and in making his choice he will be justified by this principle of the double effect. He is not doing evil that good may come. But the moralist remains adamant that a sinful action cannot be made good just because it will have good consequences. He thus closes the door firmly on that way out of moral difficulty. If he did not, wholesale lying and stealing and sexual immorality and many other evil deeds could be justified.

What are we to say about the performing of a good act if its immediate consequences are likely to be bad. For example, it is a good thing that parents should take their children to church with them. Suppose, however, that the immediate effect is to create in them a distaste for churchgoing? Should the parents force their children to go to church? The answer must be to say that this is a question of practical wisdom rather than of morals. If, after serious thought, the parents conscientiously decide not to press the matter, or vice versa, no moralist would condemn them, although he might question their wisdom. In general, it must be said that if an action is in itself good, it is unlikely to have evil consequences. For example, to tell the truth is good. To tell the truth to a dying person is certainly good. If the immediate effect of so doing is to shorten the life of that person, the action must not be judged to be blameworthy. The moralist is entitled to argue that if an act is good in its nature it cannot have morally bad consequences. It should always be remembered, however, that for an act to be good, it requires something more than good motives. It is only too true that an act performed with the best of motives may have very bad immediate consequences.

Finally, there are the remote consequences of an act. Here again, we should draw a distinction, viz. between foreseeable and unforeseeable consequences. Only the former, which may result some time after the act is performed, come into consideration. We may call them less remote, which an ordinary person could reasonably be expected to foresee. Thus a normal individual should be able to foresee that if he drinks six double whiskys in a row, it will have an adverse effect on his driving for some time after he leaves the public house. A young couple who have intercourse without the use of contraceptives could not reasonably plead that they did not foresee the birth of a child as a less remote consequence of the act. Nevertheless, we are prone to deceive ourselves too easily when it comes to recognising the consequences of our actions. The charwoman is apt to say of the broken dish which she handled too roughly: 'It came to pieces in my hand.' Similarly, Aaron pleaded innocence after fashioning the molten calf: 'I cast it into the fire and there came out this calf' (Exod. 32.24).

The moral theologian, therefore, is justified in holding the individual responsible for the less remote consequences of his actions but not for those which are more remote. These are too distant to be taken into account, and moral theology has nothing to say about them.

3

Conscience

CONSCIENCE IS fundamental in moral theology. Its authority is majestic. As Bishop Butler says: 'Had it strength as it had right, had it power, as it has manifest authority, it would absolutely govern the world.'[1] It is not relevant to our purpose here to discuss the origin of the New Testament word for conscience. It is commonly assumed by Christian writers to have been borrowed from the Stoics, and this view seems to be taken for granted by the recent Roman Catholic writer Bernard Häring in *The Law of Christ*. He does not appear to have read C. A. Pierce's book, *Conscience in the New Testament*, in which the strong objections to this assumption are pointed out. Pierce thinks that the term is derived from the general usage of *sunoida* and its compounds and analogues in the Greek-speaking world in the time of S. Paul, who (he claims) is responsible for introducing the term into Christian theology.[2]

It is, however, not the actual word *suneidesis* which is important here, for it is agreed that no equivalent is to be found in the Old Testament where (as often in the New Testament also) the word 'heart' (*lebh*) is used to denote this activity of the mind. What is important and what concerns us now is the basic conception which underlies the use of these words, and here there is to be found no

[1] Sermon II on *Human Nature*.
[2] C. A. Pierce: *Conscience in the New Testament* (1958), p. 16.

surer guide than the father of modern Anglican moral theology, Robert Sanderson (1587–1662). In his masterly lectures on *Conscience and Human Law* delivered in 1647 he has subjected the conception of conscience to a detailed scrutiny, which has never been surpassed by any moral theologian. The more longwinded treatment by his contemporary, Jeremy Taylor, is far less lucid. Indeed, the intolerable prolixity of the latter's style largely vitiates his moral theology. It has been mercilessly pilloried by Newman. 'What an array of quotations, anecdotes, similes and good sayings strung upon how weak a thread of thoughts! Turn, for example, to his *House of Feasting* which sets about proving nothing short of this, that "plenty and pleasures of the world are not proper instruments of felicity" and "that intemperance is its enemy". One might have thought it difficult either to dispute or to defend so plain a proposition; but Taylor continues to expound upon it twenty closely printed pages, not of theology or metaphysics but of practical exhortation. After quoting Seneca upon the spare diet of Epicurus and Metrodones, and a Greek poet, he demonstrates that plenty and pleasure are not natural or suitable to us, by the help of Horace, Epicurus, Seneca, Maximus Tyrius, Socrates, Juvenal, Lucian and two or three authors besides. Next he maintains that intemperance is the enemy of felicity; and for this purpose he appeals to St. Austin, Juvenal many times, Persius, Menander, Xenophon, Euripides, Plutarch, Horace, Pliny, Socrates, St. Chrysostom, Epicurus, Timotheus, Apuleius, Aristophanes, Diogenes, Plotinus, Porphyry, Prudentius, Clement of Alexandria, Horace, Plato, Pythagoras, Jamblichus, Alcaeus and Theophrastus. Having taken these means to settle the point, he proceeds to the important practical task of describing the measures of our eating and drinking between "intemperance" and "scruples". I am almost ashamed to trespass upon your indulgence, Gentlemen, with a fresh catalogue of names; yet I should not do justice to the marvellous availableness of this writer's erudition for unfolding truisms and proving proverbs unless I told you that to this new subject he devotes near a dozen pages more, using for his purpose not any common-sense principles or clear broad rules, but Juvenal, St. Chrysostom, Antidamus, Terence, St. Ambrose, Martial, Dio, Seneca, Homer, Aristotle, Horace, Boethius and others, leaving the subject much as he found it.'[1]

We begin, therefore, by summarising Sanderson's teaching on this subject, before passing on to consider modern attacks on the validity of the whole conception of conscience. It is surely incumbent on the moral theologian today to do this. It is hardly sufficient to dismiss Freud's teaching on the subject in thirteen lines, as, for example, Häring[2] does in the book to which reference has already been made.

Sanderson begins by saying: 'It is to be lamented, that mankind should engage so eagerly in the pursuit of less important knowledge and yet remain perfectly in the dark and ignorant as to the concerns of their own Consciences, especially since they can never find a more faithful Adviser, a more active Accuser, a severer Witness, a more impartial Judge, a sweeter Comforter, or a more inexorable Enemy.'[3] He then proceeds to give his definition of Conscience as follows: 'A Faculty or Habit of the Practical Understanding, which enables the Mind of Man, by the use of Reason and Argument to apply the light which it has to particular Moral Actions.'[4]

Sanderson next discusses the New Testament word, *suneidesis*, and its Latin equivalent, *conscientia*, from which our English term, conscience is derived. He says that the

[1] J. H. Newman: *Discourses on the Scope and Nature of University Education* (1852), pp. 221–3.

[2] B. Häring: *The Law of Christ* (E.T.), Vol. 1, p. 142.

[3] *Op. cit.* (ed. C. Wordsworth 1877), p. 1.   [4] *Ibid.*, p. 3.

term indicates knowledge. This, he says, can be understood in two ways. It can be taken to refer to the fact that in moral judgements the individual is conscious that he is passing not simply his own opinion but is passing judgement with Another, who is God. Alternatively it can be taken to mean the conjunction of one kind of knowledge with another—i.e. the knowledge of general principles together with the knowledge obtained by applying these to individual cases. It is in accordance with this idea that conscience has been divided into *synteresis*, which supplies the general moral laws and *conscientia* which applies them to particular cases. Sanderson points out that both these ways of understanding the word *suneidesis* are appropriate.

Following upon this is a discussion of the Aristotelian division of the human mind into powers, habits and acts, in relation to conscience. To a modern reader this will not make much appeal. The important point to notice here is that in saying that conscience is an 'Innate habit' he is making it clear, first, that conscience is not simply something acquired, like an ordinary habit—as, for example, Freud would say—and, secondly, that, on the other hand, it has to be trained and educated. Having said this, Sanderson adds that conscience is concerned with individual moral acts. He recognises the existence of acts which are morally indifferent, a fact which has been disputed by some. He writes: 'Conscience is full of eyes, she looks every way, and searches into all things; she sees clearly what is to come; and if you are rushing into Sin, she gives you fair warning, and advises you against it. She beholds you in the very Act of Sinning, and then she murmurs and plucks you back; she gnaws, pricks and belabours you, in order to keep you back; she reflects upon what is past, and when the Guilt of Sin is upon you she reproves, stings, accuses, condemns and torments you. On the contrary, she

incites you to good and laudable actions; in the execu-
tion of them, she persuades, soothes and encourages you,
and afterwards she applauds and protects you, and fills
your breast with serenity and peace.'[1] Conscience, he
says, is a Witness, a Judge and a Guide. He concludes
this part of his exposition by commenting on the significant fact 'the very things we see and tread upon, that are
obvious to our senses and understanding, that are within
the reach of the most ignorant mechanic, which the most
uneducated person thinks he apprehends, and, *in his way*,
certainly does, are yet far out of the reach of the most
acute philosophers, and the most penetrating intellects
have been puzzled in the disquisition of them. *Time, place,
motion*, what man is there, how illiterate soever, who does
not think that he fully conceives the Nature of these
things? and yet we know that the "*Profound*, the *Subtle*,
the *Angelic*, the *Seraphic* Doctors" for many ages past
have entered the lists, and are yet fatiguing themselves
upon these very subjects: and after so much toil and dust,
the Nature of them remains still unexplained and
undetermined. "I live in Time, and write about it, and
yet I know not what Time is", says St. Austin.'[2]

Such, then, according to Sanderson, is the nature of
conscience. Its obligation, however, has a double aspect,
viz. active and passive. In other words, it both obliges and
is itself bound. This (Sanderson argues) involves the
existence of some rules by which conscience is bound, or,
at any rate, some ultimate authority, which stands above
it. There are four degrees of such authority which lays an
obligation upon the conscience. The first and chiefest of
these is Almighty God Himself. He quotes S. James:
'There is one Lawgiver, who is able to save and to
destroy' (S. James 4.12). Only he who knows the inward
motions of the conscience has the power to prescribe a
law to it. This is indicated by the fact that Conscience

[1] *Ibid.*, p. 21.   [2] *Ibid.*, p. 27.

seems to 'stand in the middle between God and man.'
The second Rule of Conscience is to be found in the light
that lighteneth every man. He here quotes S. Paul's
words about the Gentiles who know not the Jewish Law
being a law unto themselves (Romans 2. 14,15).

The third Rule of Conscience is Holy Scripture, which
is the adequate Rule of Faith. The last and fourth degree
of the Rule of Conscience is the Will of God, in whatever
manner it may be revealed; but, of course, it must be
revealed if it is to be binding. Thus, under God (Sanderson teaches), there is the light of the mind, which he calls
the light innate; the written Word of God, or the light
infused or imparted; the will of God however made
known, or the light acquired. He sums this up as the
light of Nature, the light of Scripture and the light of
Doctrine.

The light of Nature—or, to give it the usual title, the
Natural Law—'consists of many practical principles',
which, however, can be reduced to two precepts: Good
is to be done and Evil is to be avoided. But certain
secondary principles may be derived (though with less
certainty) from these two. These are such as the following.
Parents are to be honoured, children to be brought up,
the life of our neighbour to be preserved, a pledge to be
restored.

Such is the nature of conscience as Sanderson describes it, and it has never been more clearly and succinctly expounded. He was, however, writing long before
the days of the Freudian revolution in psychology, which
has had a good deal to say about the claims of conscience
and the validity of its judgements. The moral theologian
today must come to terms with this new teaching. Unless
he can validate the claims of conscience in the face of it,
he must eventually go out of business. It is not enough to
dismiss Freud in a few lines. We must, therefore, turn
aside to this task before proceeding any further.

During his long life Freud's opinions underwent many changes. Some of these were due to genuine advances in the understanding of the working of the mind which characterise the work of this brilliant thinker. Some of them, on the other hand, were due to Freud's propensity to giving rein to rather wild speculations. In assessing his theories it is of great importance, therefore, to be able to separate the precious from the vile. Some of these theories rest on a rather slender substratum of fact, to say the least; and this is certainly the case with some of what he has to say about the working of conscience and its authority.

In the year 1932, only six years before his death, Freud wrote his *New Introductory Lectures on Psycho-Analysis*. Unfortunately he was unable to deliver them as lectures owing to his physical disablement due to the horrible disease which was in a comparatively short time to cause his death. In these lectures Freud developed his theory of the super-ego which he had advanced many years before, and he did so in such a way as to make it even more damaging to the Christian doctrine of the authority of conscience. It will be remembered that Freud had derived his theory of the super-ego from his dealings with psychotic (i.e. insane) patients, who were suffering from delusions that they were all the while being subjected secretly to hostile observation which threatened them with punishment. 'I formed the idea', he tells us, 'that the separating off of an observing function from the rest of the ego might be a normal feature of the ego's structure, and I was driven to investigate the further characteristics and relations of the function which had been separated off in this way. The next step is soon taken. The actual content of the delusion of observation makes it probable that the observation is only a first step towards conviction and punishment so that we may guess that another activity of this function must be what we call conscience. There is hardly anything that we separate off from our ego so regularly as our conscience and so easily set over against it.'[1]

Freud attempted to show that this super-ego, as he called it, comes into being in the case of normal persons by a process which he calls 'introjection' whereby the individual takes within his own psyche the thoughts and wishes of those set in authority over him in his early years, especially his parents. Sometimes this super-ego can be almost impossibly harsh and severe—notably in patients suffering from melancholia. This process of introjection is due to the psychological mechanism which Freud calls 'identification' which, as is well known, is especially prominent in young children, who often in their play openly 'identify' themselves with mummy or daddy or some other person. The super-ego is, therefore, according to Freud, nothing more than a particularly successful instance of identification, this being due to the fact that when the Oedipus Complex passes away it leaves a strong super-ego as a kind of precipitate. Consequently the super-ego also activates what Freud calls the ego-ideal. In the case of groups which depend upon a leader, the latter dominates the super-egos of all the members of the group. Where children have been very strictly brought up, Freud argues, they suffer from a strict super-ego. Indeed, the same may even hold good if they have not been severely brought up, because they may have introjected the harsh super-ego of their parents from which the latter have reacted. Such is the perversity of the things of the mind!

We may pause at this point, before proceeding further with the Freudian account of conscience, to assess the position. There can be no doubt that in his teaching about the super-ego Freud has lighted upon a veridical psychological experience, which is common to us all. The

[1] *Op. cit.* (E.T.), p. 81.

phenomena of introjection and identification are genuine psychological phenomena with which we are all familiar. A harsh super-ego may lead to severe mental illness and breakdown. This has been abundantly established in clinical experience. This means that, assuming the existence of conscience, as moral theology understands it, its voice may be perverted and blurred by pathological factors. But it is quite another thing to assert, as Freud asserts, that conscience can be reduced to the super-ego without remainder. Freud provides no evidence for this at all. He assumes, in an airy way, that children[1] 'are notoriously amoral' and, therefore, that conscience is not there in the beginning. If, however, he had carefully investigated the evidence, he would have found that this is not true. The small child is not amoral. There is rooted in the mind of the smallest child the sense of fair play and justice, which is the basis of the moral law. Every parent knows this. It is not something which is taught to the child. Indeed it is hard to see how it could be taught this. It is innate; and when the child begins to play games with other children and to formulate and follow the rules of the game, the latter are dependent on this. M. Piaget, who has written at length about this,[2] and who recognises the importance of these rules for the understanding of the moral outlook of the child, has failed to see the full significance of this. To say that the young child is non-moral and without what we call conscience is simply untrue; and, if it is untrue, this means that Freud's attempt to base conscience on the super-ego has failed.

Let us, however, return to Freud's exposition. Thus far the psyche has been divided into the ego and the super-ego. This, however, Freud came to see, is not a sufficient account of the matter, inasmuch as parts of both of these are unconscious. So we cannot call that part of the mind which is neither ego nor super-ego the unconscious *tout*

[1] *Ibid.*, p. 84. [2] J. Piaget: *The Moral Judgement of the Child* (1965), *passim.*

court, since the characteristic of unconsciousness is not peculiar to it. Therefore, Freud adopted the term the Id, to denote this third region of the psyche, which is mainly inaccessible to us, but is the seat of instinctual energy, knowing no values, and no morality, being governed entirely by what Freud calls the pleasure-principle. Thus the ego is placed in a truly difficult position. It has to try to serve three masters, the super-ego, the id and the external world.

In his earlier theorisation Freud had postulated two basic instinctual drives, viz. those of sex (using the term in the wide Freudian sense) and those of self-preservation; but he now rejects this and has completely altered his view of instinctual life as it is found in the id. Regarding 'instinct' as a sum of energy forcing its way in a particular direction, he thinks of instinctual drives as being subject to what he calls 'repetition-compulsion'. He was led to this, in the first place, by the remarkable tendency, which is constantly found in dreams, to return to the past and reiterate past experiences, which (it might have been supposed) the patient would often rather have left behind. Something of the same kind characterises the science of embryology. Supposing, Freud argues, that originally life arose from inanimate matter, and that at the same time a tendency (or instinct) arose to abolish life and return to the inorganic state of things, this would account for this tendency. So Freud was led to postulate two basic instinctual drives, that of Eros, or sex, and that of Death or destruction or aggression. On this assumption, he thinks, we have an explanation of the strange sexual phenomenon familiar to us as masochism, which, on this theory, will be more fundamental than its counterpart, aggressive sadism. In the masochist the death instinct has the upper hand.

What bearing, it may be asked, has all this on the theory of conscience? According to Freud, it has a vital bearing. It explains the pathological phenomenon which is the bane of the psychiatrist, viz. the unconscious desire for punishment, which plays a part in all neurotic disease. This is, to use Freud's expression, 'like the prolonging of the conscience into the unconscious', having the same origin as conscience, corresponding to a piece of aggressiveness which has been internalised and incorporated into the super-ego. This setting up of the super-ego, which makes the dangerous aggressive tendencies its own, is like introducing a garrison into a province on the brink of rebellion, as Freud expresses it.

Thus, we see, Freud's latest theory of the constitution of the psyche makes conscience appear to be even more debased, although, indeed even on this view, it is necessary.

These latest theorisings of Freud have not by any means carried conviction even to all his professed disciples. Indeed, the argument on which the whole theory of the death instinct turns, is a good example of the slipshod nature of some of Freud's thinking. Even his ardent disciple, Ernest Jones,[1] has been compelled to point out that what Freud calls 'repetition-compulsion' on which the whole theory is first based is quite a different thing from restoring a *previous* state of affairs, which is what the postulation of the death instinct demands. It is safe to say, therefore, that this part of Freud's teaching will soon take its place in the limbo of forgotten theories. Certainly no moral theologian need allow himself to be unduly perturbed by its bearing on the authority of conscience. We shall return to this question of the nature of moral consciousness later.

The moral theologian, therefore, accepts the manifest authority of the human conscience, and in so doing he agrees with the normal individual who does the same. For the most part, it is only the ultra-sophisticated who

[1] Ernest Jones: *The Life and Work of Sigmund Freud* (Pelican Books, 1961), p. 508.

have abandoned entirely the authority of conscience. But in maintaining the authority of the individual conscience, the average person is inclined to make an assumption which the moral theologian cannot accept, and that is the infallibility or virtual infallibility of the individual conscience. He thus assumes that, provided a person does not too flagrantly disobey his conscience all is well with him. This, however, is not the case. It is true that the individual conscience is inviolable—that is to say, it cannot rightly be forced, and must be obeyed. But unfortunately it is also true that it may err and be mistaken. That is why it is a serious, if not uncommon mistake to speak of conscience as being the voice of God. It is nothing of the kind. It is the capacity of the individual for hearing the voice of God, and this is something entirely different. Conscience, in fact, may be likened to a receiving set for hearing the divine voice, and this set may, and often does, get out of order. It is one of the tasks of moral theology to expound the various types of disorder to which the human conscience is subject.

AN ERRING CONSCIENCE

First of all, we must treat of an erring conscience. This is defined by Jeremy Taylor as follows: An erroneous Conscience commands us to do what we ought to omit; or to omit what we ought to do, or to do it otherwise than we should. This, unfortunately, is a situation which is by no means uncommon. Indeed, we meet it on every side. In the special conditions of Anglicanism, as we have studied them, error in the conscience is specially likely to arise. Nevertheless, moral theology teaches that even an erring conscience must be obeyed. Jeremy Taylor says: 'Indeed, the error brings in no direct obligation but that it be discovered and laid down: but so neither can it hinder but that conscience shall still retain the power that God hath given it, directly and principally; that is, that it be the man's rule and guide; for the fallacy that runs through all the objections, is this—that the erring conscience is in its obligation considered as erring. Now it does not bind, as erring, but as conscience; that is, not by its error, but by its nature, and the power of God, as being the reporter and record of his commands.'[1]

How, then, may conscience err and mislead? The answer is, through ignorance; and this ignorance may be of two kinds: ignorance of what is right, or of law, and ignorance of fact. The latter kind of ignorance does not raise any theoretical difficulties. If, for instance, a Nazirite were to pick up hastily a cup of white wine, thinking it to be water, until it was too late, his action would not be blameworthy. If I get up an hour late in the morning, having made a mistake as to the time, I act wrongly, but without blame, through ignorance of fact. Ignorance of what is right, however, is a very different matter and raises some difficult problems. As we saw in the previous chapter, in matters of civil law it is held that ignorance of the law is no excuse. If that were to be allowed, it would afford a too easy way out for the dishonest person. Whenever he was caught breaking the law he could excuse himself by pleading that he was not aware that he was infringing the law. But when the moral theologian is considering infringements of the moral law, he is ready to concede that there are occasions when ignorance must be allowed to excuse. For instance, a person who had never heard the name of Christ could hardly be blamed for not obeying Christ's teaching. Or, to take a different kind of example, a Christian who had never heard about fasting Communion could not be blamed for totally ignoring it. This being the case, moral theology has to draw a distinction between two kinds of ignorance of the law, viz. culpable and inculpable. The former is called vincible and is inexcusable. The latter is said to be

---

[1] *Ductor Dubitantium*, Book I, Chap. 3, Rule 2.

E

invincible and to exempt from blame a person even when
he is performing a bad action. It is clearly a matter of the
utmost practical importance that the moral theologian
should be able to point quite clearly to the conditions
which constitute a person 'innocently ignorant', to use
Jeremy Taylor's expression. We have already said something on the subject in the previous chapter, but we may
very briefly for convenience summarise the question here.

The plea of invincible ignorance is subject to the
following restrictions:

First, it cannot apply to any fundamental moral
principles. Secondly, it cannot apply to a person in
connexion with the knowledge required of him in his
professional capacity.

Thirdly, if a person is to plead invincible ignorance, his
ignorance must be *complete*. If there is the slightest doubt
in his mind as to whether what he is about to do is right,
he cannot plead invincible ignorance. He must set about
resolving his doubts by making the necessary enquiries.

It will be clear, from what has been said, that the
implications of the doctrine of invincible ignorance are
wide, as Bishop Kirk indicated in his book *Ignorance,
Faith and Conformity*. We need not concern ourselves with
these now. But there is one practical pastoral question of
some moment which arises and which may confront the
priest at any time. It is this. If a person is known by him
to be acting wrongly, as he believes, but in a state of
invincible ignorance, has he the moral obligation to
enlighten him? For example, in the Roman Catholic
Church not so long ago, and perhaps even now, the
priest in the confessional was tempted, and, it would
seem, yielded to the temptation to leave a penitent
suspected by him of using contraceptive devices in
(apparently) invincible ignorance. Was the priest right
to act thus? Jeremy Taylor, dealing with this question,
says: 'If the error be invincible, and the consequent of the

persuasion be consistent with the state of grace, the error must be opened, according to prudent considerations relating to the person and his affairs. So that the error must rather be suffered than a grievous scandal, or an intolerable, or a very great inconvenience.' To illustrate his point he cites the following story. 'A gentleman did ignorantly lie with his mother; she knew it, but intended it not, till for her curiosity and in her search whether her son intended it to her maid, she was surprised and gotten with child. She perceiving her shame and sorrow hasten, sent her son to travel many years; and he returned not until his mother's female birth was grown to be a handsome, pretty maiden. At his return he espies a sweet faced girl in the house, likes her, loves her, and intends to marry her. His mother conjured him by all that was sacred and profane that he should not, saying "She was a beggar's child, whom for pity's sake she rescued from the streets and beggary and that he should not by dishonouring his family make her die with sorrow." The gentleman's affections were strong and not to be mastered, and he married his own sister and his own daughter. But now the bitings of the mother's conscience were intolerable, and to her confessor she discovered the whole business within a year or two after this prodigious marriage, and asked whether she were bound to reveal the case to her son and daughter, who now lived in love and sweetness of society, innocently though with secret misfortune which they felt not.' The confessor wisely told her to say nothing, and that is the end of this highly improbable story. But it serves to illustrate the point at issue. It is also worth while saying that if artificial insemination gets going, as some would wish, cases of this kind might very easily arise.

The question of invincible ignorance leads on naturally to another allied question, and that is the education of the conscience. The average person seems to be hardly aware of this. He recognises, as we have seen, that one must obey one's conscience, but he seldom thinks that he has a duty to see that his conscience is enlightened. Yet surely there is a duty here. How far does this duty carry us? There is no short and simple answer to this question. All that can be said is that every Christian should be aware that, even when his conscience is 'clear' concerning any proposed course of action, he should obtain the best advice available to him, if there is the slightest doubt in his mind as to the rightness of his action.

A SCRUPULOUS CONSCIENCE

The next fault of conscience to be considered is scrupulosity. Here we may take Jeremy Taylor as our chief guide. He is at his very best in his handling of this difficult problem, and, when we consider that he was writing before the days of scientific psychology, his insight into the question is truly remarkable. He describes the nature of a scruple as follows: 'Scruple[1] is a little stone in the foot: if you set it upon the ground, it hurts you: if you hold it up, you cannot go forward: it is a trouble when the trouble is over, a doubt when doubts are resolved; it is a little party behind a hedge, when the main army is broken and the field cleared: and when the conscience is instructed in its way, and girt for action, a light trifling reason, or an absurd fear, hinders it from beginning the journey, or proceeding in the way, or resting at the journey's end.'[2] Before the days when the 'unconscious' had been uncovered he discerned that scrupulosity was rooted in irrational fears. He says: 'A scrupulous conscience does not take away the proper determination of the understanding; but it is like a woman handling of a frog or a chicken which, all their friends tell them, can do them no hurt, and they are

[1] From Latin *scrupulum*.
[2] *Ductor Dubitantium*, Book I, Chap. 6, Rule 1.

convinced in reason that they cannot, they believe it and know it; and yet when they take the little creature into their hands, they shriek and sometimes hold fast, and find their fears confuted, and sometimes they let go, and find their reasons useless.'[1] He truly adds: 'Fear is the disease, and that alone is infinite; and, as it commences oftentimes without cause, so it proceeds without limit.'[2] 'This disease is most frequent in women, and monastic persons, in the sickly and timorous, and is often procured by excess in religious exercises, in austerities and disciplines, indiscreet fastings and pernoctations in prayer, multitude of human laws, variety of opinions, the impertinent talk and writings of men that are busily idle.'[3]

Thus Taylor shrewdly observes that a scrupulous conscience is a diseased conscience. It is, in fact, a form of what is known today as obsessional neurosis, which every psychiatrist knows to be one of the most stubborn forms of psychoneurosis to treat. It is rooted in an unconscious sense of guilt which the victim (for he or she is a victim) tries to compensate by his hyper-sensitivity of conscience or by performing compulsive acts, like Lady Macbeth trying to wash the stains away. Writing of this condition Henderson and Gillespie say: 'There is in the obsessional neurosis regression to the anal-sadistic stage of libido development, at which there has been a developmental fixation. Memories of early traumata and difficulties at that stage, either spontaneously or because they are revived associatively by some contemporary experience, tend to return to consciousness. The ideas and emotions, often aggressive, are of a kind intolerable to the patient's super-ego and in relation to this the affect is usually one of reproach. The ego has to defend itself and tries to keep the intolerable ideas out of consciousness by substituting other ideas, indifferent in themselves. In the compulsive variety of the illness, not ideas but acts are

---

[1] *Ibid.*, Rule 2. [2] *Ibid.*, Rule 5. [3] *Ibid.*, Rule 1.

substituted. What maintains the substituted ideas or acts in consciousness is the effect of reproach, which the patient does not succeed in getting rid of when he treats the intolerable ideas in this way: the reproach attaches itself to the substituted ideas or acts.'[1]

Taylor shows equal wisdom and insight when he proceeds to give his advice as to the way in which this malady should be treated. He was writing long before the days of scientific psychiatry—although psychiatry is still far more an art than a science—but his advice still holds good, since even those who are able to afford the time and the money to have recourse to a medical psychologist cannot expect too much from that source. Taylor begins by saying: 'This is the right course in the matter of a scruple; proceed to action; and as the reason or the fear in the scruple was not inducement enough to begin, so neither to leave off.'[2] He rightly warns us of the importance of weighing our actions before we perform them, so that, *après coup*, we are more likely to be able to convince ourselves that we acted conscientiously. As Taylor very sensibly says, a person can only do his best and leave the result to God. It is just this that the man or woman afflicted with scrupulosity finds it almost impossibly difficult to do. That is why, as Taylor says, he badly needs a spiritual counsellor or guide whose godly advice he must school himself to follow. Otherwise he will go round and round in circles, his conscience becoming more and more dizzy so that he scarcely knows whether he is standing on his head or his heels. He is so distracted by his scruples that he has no time to lead a normal life. It sometimes happens that he becomes obsessed by some saying, or text from the Bible, which will dominate his whole life and make it a misery. I remember (for example) a priest whose whole life was made a torment

---

[1] Henderson and Gillespie: *Textbook of Psychiatry* (9th edn., revised by Sir David Henderson and Ivor R. C. Batchelor), p. 165.   [2] *Ibid.*, Rule 2.

by the words of S. Paul: 'Whatsoever is not of faith is sin', which words went round and round in his mind until they made his life a hell: and another case, where the words were: 'His honour rooted in dishonour stood.'[1]

Among the advices which Taylor gives to the scrupulous person are the following.[2] (1) He must 'rudely throw away' all argument. (2) He 'must fly to God by prayer and fasting'. Taylor does not here perhaps recognise sufficiently the almost impossible difficulty of this. At such times the scrupulous person must content himself with doing the best he can, impressing upon himself that God does not judge us by our poor performance but by the fact that we are doing our best. (3) He must avoid all excesses either in mortification or prayer, which are attempts to bolster up the ego in such a way as to defeat his own object. (4) He 'must take care that his religion be as near as he can to the measures and usages of common life. . . . Let us take care that our religion be like our life, not done like pictures, taken when we are dressed curiously, but looking as the actions of our life are dressed. . . . For some men mortify their natures rather than their vicious inclinations or their evil habits.' They think that they are denying *themselves* but they are not. Thus, for example, there are those who give up sugar in Lent as a form of self-denial, and who forget, as Archbishop Temple said, that in fact they may be only denying sugar and not self. (5) The scrupulous person must be careful to avoid making vows and promises, which may engender more scruples. In short, 'That religion is best which is incorporated with the actions and common traverses of our life; and as there will be some foolish actions, so there will be matter for repentance; let this humble us, but not amaze or distract us.'

[1] Tennyson: *The Idylls of the King*, Lancelot & Elaine, line 869.
[2] Doctor Dubitantium, Book I, Chap. 6, Rule 5.

A DOUBTFUL CONSCIENCE

Conscience is the guide and director of human conduct. Plainly, if it is doubtful and hesitant, it is failing in its essential function, and is of little use. 'If the trumpet give an uncertain sound, who shall prepare himself to the battle?'[1]

Four main kinds of doubt may be specified. Negative Doubt and Positive Doubt; Doubt of Fact and Doubt of Law. The first of these, Negative doubt, arises when the evidence required to settle a doubt is, for any reason, unobtainable. Jeremy Taylor gives as an example, doubt whether the number of the stars is odd or even. Another example might be whether, as an infant, I ever passed a day without crying. In practical affairs, doubt of this kind is of little consequence. Positive doubt arises when the arguments pro and con are delicately balanced; for example, when the question of the legitimacy of taking a risk arises. Plainly this must not be done in matters of life and death or grave consequence; but in lesser matters it is sometimes hard to decide. All that can be said here is that the matter must be left to the conscience of the individual to act for the best as it appears to him.

Turning to the other pair of distinctions between different kinds of doubt, doubts of fact, which are not of the negative kind, raise little difficulty. They can be easily resolved either by observation or enquiry. But it is very different concerning doubts of law. In civil law, ignorance of the law cannot be pleaded; the door of dishonesty would be too wide open. But the same does not apply in the case of conscientious doubt for the simple reason that the moral theologian is able to assume that he is dealing with *conscientious* doubt based on genuine ignorance of how far the law is binding in a particular case. Instances of this kind are the source of some of the most intricate

[1] 1. Corinthians 14.8 (AV).

and difficult of moral problems, and lead us into the field of what is known as casuistry. This is a matter of such supreme importance that it must have a chapter to itself.

Before concluding the present chapter, however, it will be worth while to consider briefly certain maxims which the moral theologian can use in trying to solve problems of doubt. The most important of these are the following:

1. *In dubio standum est pro eo, pro quo stat praesumptio:*
2. *Melior est conditio possidentis;*
3. *In dubio standum est pro valore actus;*
4. *Delictum non praesumitur, sed probari debet;*
5. *In dubio praesumptio est pro superiore.*

The first of these, to the effect that in cases of doubt one must take one's stand on the side of presumption, is really the basis of all the other maxims. Thus the maxim *melior est conditio possidentis*, or, as we say, possession is nine points of the law, means that the initial presumption is in favour of the possessor. In cases of conscientious doubt the opinion hitherto held is regarded as the opinion in possession. Thus, for example, suppose the case of a person who has been accustomed to play bridge for money being assailed by doubts as to the legitimacy of this. Hitherto he has had no scruples and this therefore is the opinion in possession, and is presumed to be right until he has been convinced it is wrong. Until then he can lawfully continue to play for stakes. This maxim is one of wide application and of great practical importance. The third maxim, *In dubio standum est pro valore actus*, means that, if we have performed an act in good faith, subsequent doubts do not invalidate that action until certainty is attained. For example, a religious, having made his or her vows, must accept them as binding until he, or she, is convinced that they were made without real understanding of what was involved. The act itself must be taken as witness that the situation was understood. Another example would be provided by the making of marriage vows. Unless it is positively proved otherwise, the fact of these vows having been made must be taken as implying that the parties understood what they were doing. The next maxim, *Delictum non praesumitur, sed probari debet*, is the recognised principle that a person is presumed innocent until he has been proved to be guilty. The final maxim, in favour of the superior, might, especially in these days, be regarded as open to question. But all the other maxims are of great practical value in resolving a doubtful conscience. At such times it is of great importance to resolve the doubt as soon as possible. There are times when it is better to act mistakenly than to go on dithering.

4

Casuistry and Modern Problems

WE NOW have to consider the question of casuistry in Anglican moral theology, and the Anglican approach to specific outstanding moral problems of our times.

The word 'casuistry' has gained rather a bad name for itself, largely perhaps because of the fierce attack made upon the Jesuits by Pascal in his famous *Provincial Letters* in the seventeenth century. Pascal had no difficulty in pillorying the appallingly lax standards which some of the Jesuits followed in the confessional and outside it; and the evil reputation which casuistry gained at that time has stuck to it ever since.

In fact, however, casuistry is simply based on a principle which it is very hard to deny and which the majority of persons assume without question. The principle is this: Circumstances alter cases. This principle can only be denied if we are prepared to take the extreme moral position that we must all the time aim at the maximum and never allow ourselves to 'let up', for a moment. This position is known as rigorism, and experience shows that in practice it is quite unworkable.

In order to appreciate the true meaning of casuistry, therefore, we must first consider the meaning of the rigorist position. Rigorism means that we must go 'all

out' all the time: that we must never 'let up'. At first
sight there are sayings of our Lord in the Gospels which
appear to imply this. For example, his exhortation to
the rich man to sell up all his possessions and follow him.
On the other hand, he did not say this to everybody.
Sometimes, he told those who wanted to follow him to go
home again. When Zacchaeus gave *half* his property to
the poor and repaid his debts with ample interest Christ
was satisfied. It is true that our Lord said 'Be ye perfect,
as your Father in heaven is perfect' but it is simply
begging the question to equate perfection with rigorism.
It does not necessarily imply that at all. It could equally
refer to perfect obedience to the will of God; and when
we come to see, as we shall see in a moment, the objections inherent in the rigorist position we are forced to the
conclusion that this is what it does mean.

Let us, then, subject the rigorist position to a careful
examination. First, we must observe that in much of our
life it is reasonably clear how we should act. In our
business or profession; towards our families; towards our
friends; towards our country. At least the main lines of
our conduct are clear for the majority of people. At
times, however, man is beset by doubt. How should I
act in this or that situation? Ought I to do this? Need I
do that? 'In each perplexing path of life', as the hymn
says, we are brought to a stand.

Some of these doubts and perplexities may sound
trivial in themselves. Take, for example, the spending
of our money. May I spend something on little luxuries?
The woman may ask herself: May I buy myself a new hat,
which catches my fancy although it is not essential, or
should I give the money to Oxfam? The man may ask if
he can treat himself to a few cigars at Christmas time?
What is the limit of luxury spending? What is the limit of
lawful recreation? May I drink? May I smoke? How far
can I go? To all such questions rigorism returns a

negative answer. You must not spend money on luxuries. You must not drink. You must not smoke.

At first sight this might appear to be the most Christian answer. If we deny ourselves these things, there is more to give to charity. Indeed, that is true; but the question is: must everybody abandon all luxuries? Must *everybody* take the strictest line when he or she is faced by doubt? That is the crucial question to be faced. It is beside the point to argue what great benefits result from the self-sacrifice of those who do choose to give up everything.

There can be little doubt that the Christian answer to this question is No, in spite of what some Christians have said. This was decided once for all in the very earliest days of Christianity when there arose the question of the obligation of Gentile Christians to keep the Jewish law and to submit to circumcision. There were many who argued in favour of this stricter course. It was, however, firmly negatived by the Apostolic Council, claiming to speak in the name of the Holy Spirit. It was negatived because, in the words of S. Peter, it 'puts a yoke on the necks of the disciples which neither we nor our fathers are able to bear' (Acts 15.10). In other words, life lived according to rigorist principles becomes quite intolerable. It flies in the face of common sense to say, as rigorism does say, that we can never have the benefit of the doubt. Circumstances alter cases. What it is reasonable to expect one man to do it may be quite unreasonable to ask of another. One man's meat is another man's poison, as the proverb truly says.

There is, however, a further objection to rigorism. Waiving all question of its reasonableness and practicability, experience shows that, in fact, it does not conduce to the most Christlike character. It is possible, as the author of Ecclesiastes says, to be righteous overmuch. This attitude of life tends to self-centredness and not to Christlikeness. It was the attitude of the Scribes and

Pharisees who prided themselves on going even beyond the requirements of the law. And, what is more, this attitude of mind easily leads to that diseased state known as scrupulosity, when all sense of proportion is lost, and molehills become mountains.

In the face of the impossibility of rigorism some way of meeting the difficulties raised by conscientious doubt clearly has to be found. In the Roman Church in the sixteenth century the moral theologian Bartholomew Medina succeeded to a great extent in establishing the system of casuistry known as Probabilism. This was not a novelty, for it can be traced back for centuries; but it was Medina who was chiefly responsible for establishing it as the method of casuistry in the Roman Catholic Church, as it is predominant to this day. Medina stated it thus: 'If an opinion is probable, it is lawful to follow it, although the opposite opinion is more probable. . . . An opinion is said to be probable, when we can follow it without blame and without scandal.'[1] It was found necessary to elaborate this somewhat bald statement by certain qualifications, to the effect that probabilism did not apply to cases where a certain and definite end was required, as, for example, in the case of a doctor in prescribing drugs for a patient, when no risks could be allowed, or, again, in the case of prayer and the administration of the sacraments. Apart from such cases, however, a doubtful conscience could be eased by following this principle. The question was always regarded as arising from a conflict between law and liberty. According to probabilism, in the case of serious doubt, liberty could prevail against law where a seriously grounded argument for liberty could be produced.

Probabilism, however, never took root in Anglican moral theology, and the two fathers of distinctively Anglican moral theology, viz. Robert Sanderson and

[1] See Prümmer: *Manuale Theologiae Moralis I*, p. 342.

Jeremy Taylor rejected it out of hand as tending far too much towards moral laxity and gave their support to the system of casuistry known as Probabiliorism, which asserted that in cases of conscientious doubt, the more probable opinion must prevail against the less probable. To the argument (which is still heard) that it is too often not possible to decide which course of action *is* more probably right Taylor gave a direct negative. He says; 'In matters of conscience, it is as hard to find a case so equally probable that a man shall find nothing without or within to determine him, as it is to find that which the philosophers call "temperamentum ad pondus", "a constitution so equal that no part shall excel the other".'[1]

Sanderson deals with the matter as follows:[2] He takes his stand on two propositions: (1) *In dubiis rebus potior est conditio possidentis*, i.e. possession is, as we say, nine points of the law, and (2) *In re dubia tutior pars est eligenda*. In other words, he accepts the position that problems of conscientious doubt are rightly regarded as being due to a conflict between law and liberty, but he deduces from this not probabilism but what is in effect probabiliorism. This is best explained by an example. Suppose the case of a young man who has been brought up to think that it is wrong to drink alcohol, but who is led seriously to doubt the truth of this. The belief that total abstinence is right is, so to say, in possession, and he is morally bound to follow that course unless and until he is quite satisfied that the opposite opinion is more securely founded.

But before he can proceed rightly to claim liberty of action in this matter he has to satisfy the second proposition: in cases of serious doubt the safer course has to be chosen. In other words, it is better to be safe than sorry. It is better, as far as possible, for a doubting conscience to obey than to disobey. Here Sanderson leans heavily

[1] *Ductor Dubitantium*, Book V, Chap. 4, Rule 5.
[2] *Lectures on Conscience and Human Law*, p. 178 (ed. C. Wordsworth).

towards rigorism, and does not, I think, really do justice to the intensity and even the agony of conscientious doubt.

However this may be, it is clear that Anglican moral theology has turned right away from any lax tendencies, and ever since Sanderson and Taylor it has tended to follow their lead until recent times, when the whole traditional system of casuistry has been called in question, and it has been claimed that love alone is sufficient or adequate as a guide for the doubting conscience. Our next task, therefore, must be to examine this position with some care, and to see how far it can be accepted as valid.

We may take as our starting point here what Aristotle has to say about right conduct in the second book of his Nicomachaean Ethics. He issues a warning to which some of our present-day moralists would do well to give heed. He says: 'In reasoning about matters of conduct general statements cover more ground but particular statements are more accurate, for conduct is concerned with particulars.'[1] It is easy enough to say in an airy-fairy manner that love is all that is required to solve our moral problems; but what has to be shown is exactly how this works out in practice.

Aristotle follows his own advice. He goes on to try to show how it is possible to achieve right conduct, which he sees as a mean between two extremes; but what he has to say is quite independent of this particular conception. He points out that right conduct means behaving in any given situation with 'the right person, to the right extent, at the right time, with the right intention, and in the right manner.' Clearly there is every chance of doubt creeping in here as to what these several conditions require, and it is often in practice useless to tell a person beset and plagued by doubt that all he needs is to love, and to

[1] E.N. Book II, 1117a.

treat others as he would like to be treated in such circumstances.

What is needed for the relief of conscientious doubt is, in the first instance, some rough and ready rule to which the doubter can turn; for, as Jeremy Taylor says 'in a doubting conscience the immediate cure is not to choose right but to choose at all'.[1] This, at least, Probabilism provides. So does Probabiliorism. The criterion of 'love' is not nearly so easy to apply, though it will suffice for some people and for some circumstances; but it is very far from being a generally adequate guide for the doubting conscience.

One or two examples will soon make this clear. Take the well-known case of the conscientious objector in time of war torn between love of his country and his pacifist views. To tell him to act according to love may seem to him mockery. It is his very love for his country and (perhaps) his wife and children whose lives are threatened, that is the source of his doubt. Take the case of the girl who is torn by the competing claims of a call to the mission field as a nurse and a call to nurse an invalid parent. To tell her to act in accordance with love is to mock her. Or take the well-known case of choosing between the life of the baby and the life of the mother, as, for instance, Soames Forsyte had to choose in the Forsyte Saga. To say that love will solve this doubt is futile; and many other similar cases could be quoted. One who accepted the principles of Probabilism would at least find in these cases a way of escape from the torture of a doubting conscience; and this is precisely the aim and object of casuistry. Rightly understood, it does not apply except in such circumstances. It is utterly unfair to describe it as 'a set of rules for the breaking of rules'.

Where, then, does Anglicanism stand in this matter of

[1] *Ductor Dubitantium*, Of a Doubtful Conscience, Rule VII.

casuistry today? One thing is certain, and that is that if we jettison Probabilism and Probabiliorism we must find something to put in its place. Here, again, Aristotle can perhaps help us. In discussing the problem of how to ascertain the details of right action he says that when we are faced by what appears to be a choice of evils we should choose the lesser.[1] Later on he elaborates this by saying: 'The lesser evil stands in the place of good in comparison with the greater evil, for the lesser evil is more desirable than the greater, and that which is desirable is good and that which is more desirable is a greater good.'[2]

Some moralists will not accept this position. Sanderson, for example, says that we should never choose to do wrong, and he denies that we can ever be placed in such a position as to be compelled to do what is evil.[3] Here surely he is mistaken. For example a surgeon forced to choose between the life of the mother and the life of the baby is in such a position. To refuse to act is in fact just as much an action as to perform an operation. Moreover, those who take this view fail to give due recognition to the fact that in such circumstances our first task is to release the conscience from torturing doubt.

In my view, this principle of choosing the lesser evil or what appears to be the lesser evil is an invaluable help in casuistry. Many examples could be given of its use, which unfortunately is not always recognised. A crucial example is provided by the practice of admitting divorced persons to Holy Communion although they have been denied 'remarriage' in church. There is nothing illogical here, as it is sometimes said. The action is based on the principle of choosing the lesser evil, i.e., running the risk of seeming to condone the 'marriage' rather than refilling them from the altar. The

---

[1] E.N. Book II, 1109a.   [2] E.N. Book V, 1131b.
[3] *Op. cit.*, p. 51.

lesser evil here, once chosen, becomes a good action.

Some cases which present themselves as a choice between two evils, but by no means all of them, can be dealt with by what is called in moral theology the principle of the double effect.[1] This states that where a single action has two effects, one bad and one good, it may be lawfully performed provided that only the good effect is intended. Perhaps the simplest illustration of this is a surgical operation. Every such operation is an assault upon the body, which has greater or lesser evil consequences. To make an incision in the abdomen with a knife and cut a person open, for example, or to remove a limb is an evil thing. But if the primary intention is to combat disease, the action becomes legitimate and good. There are many such cases in human life where this principle can be invoked. It has already been stated in an earlier chapter that this is not to say that the end justifies the means. That is an immoral doctrine, condemned by S. Paul (Romans 6) and repudiated by all moral theologians, and applies to two distinct actions, whereas the principle of double effect applies only to a single action with two effects, one of which is good and the other bad. Where it is a case of judging between two separate actions, therefore, the principle of the double effect is not applicable and recourse must be had to the principle of choosing the lesser of two evils.

In the end it remains true that the doubter must fall back on his own moral judgement, unless he is able to commit his conscience to the keeping of some moral authority, *e.g.* the Pope. Even then he cannot divest himself of the responsibility of deciding which moral authority to accept. It is the business of casuistry, however, to make the moral choice as clear as it can possibly be made and to reduce to the absolute minimum the area of doubt.

[1] See *supra*, p. 40.

Let us now turn our attention to various specific moral questions which are pressing at the present time in order to clarify the attitude which the Anglican moral theologian should take towards them. First, let us consider the question of contraception. Something has already been said about this in expounding the Anglican conception of moral theology, but a more systematic treatment of this vitally important question is demanded.

At the outset, it is, I think important not to equate the use of artificial contraceptive methods with 'family planning', as is so frequently the case. The two things are by no means the same. It is quite possible to 'plan' a family without having recourse to artificial methods, whether mechanical or chemical; indeed, it is obviously a Christian duty to 'plan your family'. No responsible person could advocate the bringing of children into the world entirely at random. In order, therefore, to avoid confusion of thought, we should be careful to observe this distinction. We are now concerned with the use of mechanical and chemical methods of birth-control.

During the last twenty or thirty years there has been a profound change in 'the climate of opinion' in the Church, as elsewhere, on this matter. We have already seen this reflected in the reports of the several Lambeth Conferences which have taken place during that period. Prior to this, broadly speaking, the traditional Christian opinion that the use of these methods was contrary to divine Natural Law and, therefore utterly condemned, prevailed. Today this strict view is to be found only in the teaching of the Roman Catholic Church, which has just been reaffirmed by Pope Paul VI in his recent encyclical, which states that "each and every marriage act ("quilibet matrimonii usus") must remain open to the transmission of life."[1] It is, however, an open

---

[1] *Humanae Vitae*, § 11.

secret, revealed very plainly at the recent Vatican
Council, that this teaching is rejected by many Roman
Catholic theologians, and widely ignored by the faith-
ful, confessors being forced to turn a blind eye to it.
Sooner or later the Roman Church will *officially* have
to come to terms with this deep change of opinion. Its
present inability to do so is certainly damaging to the
Papal claim that the Bishop of Rome is an infallible
guide in the matters of faith and morals. The Anglican
moralist is plainly at a great advantage over his Roman
Catholic brother; for there is no *official* Anglican
Teaching on this question.

What has led to this dramatic change of opinion?
There have been several reasons for it. First, there has
been an increasing awareness of the value and importance of *coitus* in the husband-wife relationship. It is fair
to say that this has been insufficiently recognised by the
Church in the past, perhaps because so many of those
who have been most influential in formulating the
teaching of the Church have been celibates. The cynic
may well say, what do a lot of old bachelors know about
this? Many modern Anglican theologians, who have
been married men themselves, have been in the forefront
of this argument. Secondly, and following upon this, has
been the great improvement in the methods of contraception, both mechanical and chemical. These have culmi-
nated in 'the pill' which has, at least, entirely removed the
aesthetic objection to the use of contraceptives, which
has undoubtedly weighed heavily against them in the
minds of many. This greater efficiency and security has
clearly done not a little to commend the use of these
devices. Especially is this the case with 'the pill'. But finally
it should be carefully remembered that the use of 'the pill'
raises some difficult psychological problems, apart
altogether from possible harmful physical side-effects
which it is too early to assess at present, but which are

certainly there.[1] On the psychological side, the very efficiency of this contraceptive often seems to increase a woman's sexual desire to such an extent as to embarrass some husbands and even to make them impotent. Secondly, the effectiveness of the pill can create very great difficulties for a husband whose business takes him away from home a great deal and who has any doubts or suspicions concerning the fidelity of his wife. In such circumstances the pill opens the door wide to infidelity, and may lead to great matrimonial difficulties. Evidence of this kind may lead some to think that the pill is too good to be true.

The third factor which has helped to bring about the change which we are discussing is the increased understanding of the physiology of sex whereby it is clear that the woman's part in procreation is not purely passive, as was at one time believed, but just as positive as that of the husband. In a deeper sense than was once supposed, husband and wife are 'joint heirs of the grace of life' (1 Peter 3.7). It is worth remembering that the author of these words was a married man.

Finally, and in some ways most important of all, the whole picture has been changed by what is called 'the population explosion'. This has been brought about by various causes, especially the advance of medical hygiene which has reduced infant mortality in a well-nigh miraculous manner. It is now a matter of urgency to restrain the increase of mankind, although the experts appear to differ as to the danger of doing this beyond the resources of Mother Earth, if these resources were properly husbanded. The result is that, whereas even thirty or forty years ago, the command 'Be fruitful and multiply' could be taken literally, today this is no longer possible.

---

[1] See the Reports by Dr. Richard Doll and Dr. M. P. Vessey and by Dr. W. H. Inman respectively, published in the British Medical Journal of 27 April this year, where the risks of pulmonary embolism and cerebral thrombosis ensuing are put forward and discussed. Clearly they are not negligible.

How does the Anglican moralist react to this situation? Broadly speaking, he can and does adopt one of three different positions. The first is a modification of the traditional position, based on the natural law doctrine; for few, if any, Anglicans would today accept the position of *Humanae Vitae*. They would say that, although the best method of family planning is either to use abstinence or to come together only during 'the safe period' there are many instances when these methods are impracticable, and that, when this is the case, other methods may be used by Christian man and wife in agreement; but it remains a second best. This was substantially the position taken by the majority vote in the 1930 Lambeth Conference.

The second position, taken by many Anglican moralists, is to go much further than this, and to welcome contraceptive devices as truly beneficial results of scientific research and progress. These, it is said, have liberated millions of women from the haunting fear of pregnancy, and have made it possible for the first time for what is called the 'relational' aspect of *coitus* to find adequate expression. But those who adopt this position still point to the dangers inherent in the unbridled use of contraceptives, and are deeply concerned to emphasise the great importance of 'chastity' within marriage as well as outside. This leads to the view that knowledge and possession of these devices should be strictly limited, as far as possible, to those who are married.

The third position goes the whole way. It positively glories in contraception as being one of the greatest benefits of modern medical science. It would extend the knowledge and use of it to all comers—not only to the married, and the engaged, but to all girls and young men everywhere. If these are going to cohabit, it is argued, let them at least do so without the risk of bringing unwanted children into the world and being led into the temptation to procure abortion.

What attitude is the Anglican to adopt, when he is faced by these three different opinions concerning contraception? If he tackles the problem on Probabilist principles, he can appeal to Resolution 115 of the 1958 Lambeth Conference which, while not being entirely free from ambiguity, suggests that a married couple are free to make their own judgement as to what means may be employed in family 'planning'. 'The Conference believes that the responsibility for deciding upon the number and frequency of children has been laid by God upon the consciences of parents everywhere: that this planning, in such ways as are mutually acceptable to husband and wife in Christian conscience, is a right and important factor in Christian family life and should be the result of positive choice before God. Such responsible parenthood, built on obedience to all the duties of marriage, requires a wise stewardship of the resources and abilities of the family as well as a thoughtful consideration of the varying population needs and problems of society and the claims of future generations.' This judgement, for an Anglican, is 'a probable opinion' and therefore, according to the principles of Probabilism, sufficient to relieve a doubtful conscience.

If this method of resolving doubt is unacceptable, as well it may be, recourse may be had to the principle of choosing the lesser evil. The question may be stated thus. On any understanding of contraceptives, it is a lesser evil to use them than to bring an unwanted child into the world or to throw upon a marriage the strain of prolonged abstinence. This argument would hold good for those who adopt the first of the three positions outlined above. Still more does it hold good for those who take the second view. Therefore it may be said that a careful and thoughtful use of contraceptives is not to be condemned. In those cases where another pregnancy would 'endanger the life of the wife or seriously and permanently impair her health', the argument becomes still stronger. In so far as there can be said to be an Anglican position in this matter, this may fairly be said to represent it.

We come now to a problem which is very closely allied to that which we have just been considering, and that is the question of sterilisation. Indeed, in one of its aspects it is to be regarded as a form, and the most effective form, of contraception. There are, however, other uses of sterilisation, viz. therapeutic, eugenic and punitive. Furthermore, it can be—what contraception in the usual sense of the term can never be—not only voluntary but also compulsory.

We must first observe that in recent times this problem has been considerably changed by reason of the fact that, whereas in former times the only known form of direct sterilisation was castration of the male, today it exists in two other varieties, vasectomy for the male and salpingectomy for the female, the former being, at least theoretically, a reversible process.[1] All this has to be borne in mind in any modern reassessment of the question. Traditionally in moral theology sterilisation has been unequivocally condemned on the ground that it is a mutilation of the human body which is a sin against oneself, against the community by making procreation impossible, and against God, who alone has full rights over man. There is only one set of circumstances in which this has been held lawful, viz. in the interests of the body as a whole. So Aquinas says: 'If a member of the body be diseased and so a source of corruption to the whole body, it is lawful for him whose body it is voluntarily to cut off the diseased member for the sake of the health of the whole body; for to each person is committed the care of his own health. And the same applies if this happens by the will of anybody who has the care of the

[1] It is said that this applies only to 30 or 40 per cent of cases.

person with the diseased body. Otherwise it is utterly unlawful for anybody to maim a person.'[1]

This is still the teaching of the Roman Catholic Church laid down anew in 1930 in *Casti Connubii* by Pope Pius XI and repeated by Pius XII, when he said in an address to midwives: 'Direct sterilisation, that which aims at making procreation impossible as both means and end, is a grave violation of the moral law, and therefore illicit.'[2]

Such is the traditional attitude towards sterilisation, but two considerations must be borne in mind today in considering this question. The first is that 'traditional moral theology has not been called upon to consider the extent of the obligations of parenthood under the threat of over-population', as, for instance, it occurs in India today. We quote from the Report of the Committee of the Church Assembly Board of Social Responsibility,[3] which goes on to say: 'Faced as we are by a situation in which a responsible government is pursuing, together with other ameliorative measures, a policy of persuasion for voluntary sterilisation, and asked by Christian doctors and nurses involved in the carrying out of this policy for help in deciding for themselves how far they can co-operate, we are bound to conclude that we find no grounds on which to reply in terms of an absolute negative'.[4] Clearly the question is open for re-examination.

This leads us to the second consideration which has to be remembered in the present connexion, and that is that Aquinas, in arguing for capital punishment does so by bringing in the social dimension of the problem. He claims that capital punishment is legitimised by the argument that just as in the individual body a diseased

[1] *Summa Theologica*, IIa IIae Q.65, a.i.
[2] Quoted by N. St. John Stevas in *Life, Death and the Law* (1961), p. 168, n. 3.
[3] *Sterilisation: an Ethical Enquiry* (Church Information Office, 1962), p. 25.
[4] *Op. cit.*, p. 25.

member may be removed for the good of the body as a whole, so in the body politic the criminal, if a grave danger to the same, may in like manner be removed.[1] It is this social aspect of the problem of sterilisation which has suddenly begun to loom so large, and which in the past has been totally ignored. Accordingly the authors of *Sterilisation: an Ethical Enquiry* seem to have reason on their side when they say that it is not adequate 'to discuss the morality of sterilisation in terms of a "necessity" limited to the body of the patient alone; the morality and casuistry of the act must relate to the fact that the patient's life is "incorporate" with that of his spouse, his family, and the society or body politic of which he is a member'.[2]

The result of the adoption of this wider standpoint has been to lead some Christian moralists to argue for the legitimacy of sterilisation even when the operation is not performed in the interests of the present health of the individual concerned. They would argue, for example, that it would be legitimate if performed on a woman for whom another pregnancy would be dangerous. And many would argue in favour of voluntary sterilisation for simple people living in countries shadowed by the threat of over-population where ordinary contraceptive methods would probably be inadequate. One thing is clear. Once the legitimacy of the wider social reference in this problem is accepted, sterilisation may be legitimate not only as a form of contraception or for therapeutic reasons but also for eugenic and even punitive reasons. In this case the individual is forced to make a moral choice. The kind of considerations which he should take into account in making such a decision are well stated in the Report which has already been quoted. 'Before deciding in favour of sterilisation, they will con-

---

[1] *Summa Theologica*, IIa IIae Q.64, a.2. But this smacks of totalitarianism.
[2] *Op. cit.*, p. 19.

sider whether other means are open to them: is sexual abstinence, total or periodic, possible or desirable? Or is there a contraceptive method available and acceptable? What are the present ages and state of health of the wife and of the husband? How long will it be before the wife becomes sterile by nature? The wife might be unlikely to marry again if she were widowed, in a society which does not favour the re-marriage of widows; but very probably the husband would wish to marry again if his wife were to die before he was old. And what then of his new wife's desire for and right to bear children? Assuming both operations to be irreversible, this last consideration might point to the sterilisation of the wife rather than of the husband—an operation of no great difficulty in the day or two immediately after childbirth (though that is not the best time for making a calm and careful joint decision). But if vasectomy were really reversible, this fact would strongly favour the sterilisation of the husband.'[1] To this should be added consideration of the psychological dangers attendant upon sterilisation to which reference has already been made in connexion with the contraceptive pill.

In trying to reach a conclusion, sooner or later recourse must be had to the principle of the lesser evil; but because (in the words of the Committee on the Family in the 1958 Lambeth Conference) it is 'a major and irrevocable abdication of an important area of responsible freedom' and 'has psychological and physiological consequences that are as yet unknown and unmeasured and represents as well a violation of the human body'[2] it should be undertaken only after most careful deliberation and full agreement of both parties.

Something must now be said concerning eugenic sterilisation. This is entirely disallowed by Roman Catholic moralists on the ground that it cannot be

[1] *Ibid.*, p. 31.   [2] *Op. cit.*, 2, 149.

brought under the plea that it is for the benefit of the individual body of the person sterilised. What judgement must the Anglican moral theologian make on this question? There can be no doubt—as Roman Catholic moralists are quick to point out—that the possible benefits of this process are far less than at one time was supposed to be the case. It is known that mental deficiency is reproduced not only by mental defectives themselves but also by 'carriers', who appear to be quite normal but whose body contains 'recessive' genes which will lead ultimately to mental deficiency in later generations. Since carriers far outnumber defectives, sterilisation is of very limited value here. The chief value of the sterilisation of mental defectives is that, since they are apt to make most unsatisfactory parents, they are prevented from having children whose characters they may spoil. Is this a legitimate procedure? We are here back at the problem of contraceptive sterilisation.

Finally, there is the case of what is called punitive sterilisation, to restrain 'sex maniacs' and other similar persons who are a danger to society. Here we meet with a new factor, viz. compulsory sterilisation; so far we have been concerned only with sterilisation on a voluntary basis. Some moralists hold that this rules it out completely. Bishop Barry, for example, says: 'Any attempt at compulsory sterilisation involves an infringement of human rights, and a violation of personal freedom and liberty which a Christian Ethic is bound to condemn and resist. This would also apply to any proposal for compulsory sterilisation as a penal measure.'[1] This argument, however, proves too much; it would make prisons unlawful institutions and condemn the certification of the insane. A more forcible argument against penal sterilisation is to say that it fails of its essential purpose; for sterilisation does not abate sexual desire, and may even

[1] F. R. Barry: *Christian Ethics and Secular Society* (1966), p. 262.

increase it in some cases. It can also be a positive encouragement to sexual promiscuity.

Although, therefore, it affords protection against conception through rape, it is no protection against rape itself. The weight of Christian opinion is consequently against it.

We turn now to a kindred moral problem which is a burning issue at the present time, viz. the question of abortion. It seems to be impossible to obtain accurate statistics, but there is no doubt at all that the number of abortions is very high, and this is a question which is causing grave concern to the governments of many countries, including our own. Now the British Government has just passed an Act explicitly legalising abortion for the first time, not only when the life of the mother is threatened, but also her health, whether physical or mental, or that of any existing children of her family; or if 'there is a substantial risk that if the child were born it would suffer from such physical or mental abnormalities as to be seriously handicapped'.[1] These proposals have led to great questioning and controversy, which is still far from being at an end. What guidance can Christian moral theology give to those who seek to find their way in this maze of disputation?

The problem is one of considerable difficulty, but it has been rendered more difficult than it need be by dragging in the question of the existence of the soul. This is not strictly relevant. Even those who wish to deny the existence of the soul in the unborn foetus—and I am certainly not one of them—have to admit that it is a potential human being, physically complete by the end of the twelfth week. Abortion destroys this foetus and prevents it from coming to maturity, and this is morally really no different from killing one which is full grown. To prevent something good from developing is morally

---

[1] *Abortion Act,* (1967) Section 1, sub section (1) a & b.

hardly distinguishable from destroying the end product when it has come into being. The essential problem of abortion remains the same in both cases, i.e. Is it ever legitimate deliberately to procure an abortion, and if so, in what circumstances?

The traditional Christian answer to this question is to say that abortion is always *per se* wrong, because it is an act of homicide. This is still the official teaching of the Roman Catholic Church and, judging by the pronouncements of two Lambeth Conferences, this is also the teaching of the Anglican Church, so far as it is ascertainable.

The 1930 Lambeth Conference simply said: 'The Conference further records its abhorrence of the sinful practice of abortion' (Resolution 16). In 1948 the Lambeth Conference rather surprisingly made no reference to abortion in its Resolutions, but the committee dealing with the family said: 'In the strongest terms Christians reject the practice of induced abortion, or infanticide, which involves the killing of a life already conceived (as well as a violation of the personality of the mother) save at the dictate of strict and undeniable medical necessity.'

There is clearly need for a fuller elucidation of this matter. Circumstances undoubtedly arise in which to destroy the foetus in the womb, although an evil, is the lesser of two evils; and in such circumstances Roman Catholic theologians invoke the principle of the double effect. For instance, where the pregnant mother suffers from a carcinoma of the womb, it is legitimate to remove the womb and procure thereby an abortion. Here the intention of the action is not to abort but to save the life of the mother; the attack on the *foetus* is, as it is said, *indirect*. Similarly, abortion would be approved to save the life of the mother, if that were threatened by allowing the pregnancy to run to its full term.

That is as far as traditional moral theology is prepared to go; and the difficulty today is that there are a great many seriously minded people who wish to go very much further, as do the supporters of the act of parliament already quoted. It is this fact which has led to the widespread disputations on this subject at the present time. What has the Anglican moralist to say? Is he prepared to go further than his Roman Catholic brother, further than the two Lambeth Conferences went?

In 1965 an Anglican Committee, appointed by the Church Assembly Board of Social Responsibility, which, of course, had no authority to speak for anybody except themselves, issued a Report[1] which accepted the principle that the circumstances justifying abortion should go beyond the one case in which failure to abort would jeopardise the life of the mother, holding that the condition of the mother's health and well-being, in the fullest and widest sense should be taken into consideration. If, in the opinion of two medical practitioners, this would be gravely harmed by allowing the pregnancy to run to its term, abortion should be legitimised. The Committee did not agree that the possibility of grave abnormality in the child when born or the fact that it had been conceived after rape were *per se* grounds for legitimising abortion, though clearly they would, if present, be likely strongly to influence the mother's state of mind.

The great weakness of this position is that the new criteria legitimising abortion are so vague and intangible that they could be made to authorise almost anything; and this means that in practice it must lay far too heavy a burden of responsibility on the two doctors who have to make the decision. From the point of view of the moralist the new criteria are equally unsatisfactory because of their extreme elasticity. In practice, they will open the door far too widely to the practice of abortion,

---

[1] *Abortion: An Ethical Discussion* (Church Information Office, 1965).

for the latter has now ceased to be simply a medical therapeutic act and become a social therapeutic act also. The new situation is one which is likely to strain severely the consciences of many medical men, although there is a conscience clause in the Act stating that 'no person shall be under any duty . . . to participate in any treatment authorised by this Act to which he has a conscientious objection'. In the judgement of most Christian moralists, it would be wrong to have anything to do with abortion on 'social' grounds, which lead straight to totalitarianism.

This Report, indeed, was in large measure concerned with possible legislation on this matter; and this was, perhaps, unfortunate, because moral theology is not directly concerned with the making of laws but with moral issues as such, and the Report perhaps did not sufficiently come to grips with these. And here the moral theologian is bound to say, as I should think, that in a grave matter of this kind—literally a matter of life and death—no avoidable risks should be taken. This means that it is a greater evil to risk a wrongful abortion than to risk the possibility of an abnormal birth or harm to the health of the mother.

We turn next to the consideration of artificial human insemination. In the case of animal breeding artificial insemination has been known for centuries, but it has been practised among human beings only in recent times, and, so far as the evidence goes (and it is difficult to assess this) only on a very small scale, although it is certainly increasing. It exists in two different forms, described as (a) Homologous, when the semen of the husband is used and (b) Heterologous, when the seed of a donor is utilised. The former is known as A.I.H. and the latter as A.I.D.

A.I.H. is used in cases where there is impotence in the male or inability to achieve coitus in the normal way for any reason—e.g. vaginal spasm or dyspareunia (painful

G

coitus). Whether or not this is approved morally by Christians depends partly on how the husband's semen is obtained. If it is 'assisted' by instruments into the vagina, the cervical canal or the uterus, immediately after intercourse, it is approved by all Christian moralists, including Roman Catholic moral theologians, on the ground that this is only an extension of the normal act of intercourse. But if the semen is obtained by masturbation or *coitus interruptus*, the act is condemned by the Roman Catholic Church because these actions are considered to be *per se* wrong. Probably most Anglican moral theologians would disagree with this, holding that these actions, in the changed circumstances, cease to be wrong.

It is when we come to A.I.D. that difficulties chiefly arise. This is required when there is male sterility or hereditary disease or defect in the husband. It is condemned by Roman Catholic moral theologians without qualification, following upon the condemnation of Pope Pius XI in *Casti Connubii* (1930) and Pius XII in 1949 on the ground that 'the procreation of new life can only be the fruit of marriage'.[1] A.I.D. is also condemned by the majority of Anglican moral theologians, but not by all. Those who condemn it do so for the following reasons:

1. In Great Britain it is illegal, and regarded as adulterous (see Russell *v.* Russell, House of Lords 1924). Furthermore, in law the registration of a child begotten by A.I.D. as the child of the husband, would be a contravention of the Perjury Act 1911.[2]

2. Even if it were legal, it would involve a large measure of deception, the facts being known only to the couple concerned and their medical adviser; but there are some advocates of A.I.D. who maintain that strict

---

[1] Quoted by N. St. John Stevas, *op. cit.*, p. 137, n.2.

[2] *Artificial Human Insemination*, Report of a Committee appointed by the Archbishop of Canterbury (1948), p. 40.

secrecy need not be observed. We shall consider this shortly.

3. The psychological dangers both to the 'parents' and to any child so born are so grave as to make the action unwarranted.

4. The strong desire of a wife to bear a child may well be inordinate and pathological and one to be resisted for the ultimate good of the woman herself.

Chiefly for some or all of these reasons A.I.D. is condemned by the majority of Anglican moral theologians. There are some, however, who do not find them compelling. They argue as follows. It is not satisfactory to call A.I.D. adulterous, since it is approved by both husband and wife; and to describe it so is, in the words of Dean Matthews, to adopt a 'crassly materialistic' view of the marriage union. This is, or should be (he claims) based on love, and A.I.D. involves no violation of this, but, on the contrary, is an expression of it. The husband welcomes the donor's child because of his very love for his wife. Yet, as the Report of the Archbishop's Committee argues, if A.I.D. is approved, why should not 'the concealed introduction of a child begotten by the husband but born of a woman other than the wife, whether normally or artificially by means of his services as 'donor' also be approved? It is fairly certain that it would not be. The fact is that advocates of A.I.D. on the ground that 'love' and 'personal relationships' are the basis of marriage minimise the vital importance of the family as being rooted in a physical relationship, as being, in fact, sacramental. To try to juggle with this by the manipulation of human semen is a most dangerous procedure. If 'orthodox' A.I.D. from a known (to the physician) donor is approved, why not semen taken from a 'bank' of the mixed semen of a dozen different men in order to secure complete anonymity? It is hard to see where this procedure will take us'.

We come now to the question of secrecy. As it is usually explained, complete secrecy is essential for A.I.D. only the physician concerned having knowledge of the 'donor'. Apart from the legal aspect of 'perjury' in registering the birth of a child with such parentage, the whole procedure is a deliberate act of deception. Surely this is a most unsatisfactory basis for bringing a child into the world. There is no real analogy here with the procedure of legal adoption, where the birth is correctly registered and everything is above board, the child himself in due course being informed of the facts of his birth, if the parents are wise. The only way of surmounting this grave objection to A.I.D. is to abandon secrecy. Most advocates of A.I.D. cannot face that possibility, but one of them, the Rev. Joseph Fletcher, does. He says that, just as parents of an adopted child inform him, when the right moment comes, that he is 'adopted' so the parents of an A.I.D. child should inform him that he has been 'co-opted'![1] It is hard to see the two cases as being really parallel. It is one thing to be informed that your parents are not those whom you had supposed them to be; it is another thing to be told that you were 'a test-tube baby'. The psychological shock might well prove to be devastating; and the risk of administering this shock to any child is one which it is very hard to justify. It is reasonable to say that the practice of A.I.D. must depend upon inviolable secrecy.

There is a further complicating factor in A.I.D. We have seen that it may be employed in cases where the husband has some hereditary disease or infirmity which must not be transmitted. Clearly any child born in such circumstances by A.I.D. might have to be informed of these in order to allay his fears, should they arise, as well might be the case. A very difficult situation would be created, fraught with grave psychological danger. Since

[1] Joseph Fletcher: *Morals and Medicine* (1955), p. 126.

ex hypothesi this is one of the two chief uses of A.I.D. it might become far from uncommon.

So far nothing has been said of A.I.D. practised for purely eugenic reasons, as these are totally unacceptable to the Christian conscience. They reduce sexual morality to the level of the farmyard. Thus Glanville Williams says: 'It opens the way for separating the procreative from the companionate and sexual (*sic*) elements in marriage. A woman can now choose one man as the biological father of her children, and another as her lover and companion, and the father of her children by adoption. It offers the possibility, too, of immensely increasing the number of women whom it is practicable for one man, regarded as of good stock, to fertilise.'[1]

Such degrading proposals as these need not concern us now. They would be rejected not only by all Christians but by right-minded people generally. But, as we have seen, A.I.D. in order to solve the problem of the sterile husband or that of the diseased husband who fears to transmit his disease or defects to his offspring is another question. We have seen that even in this form A.I.D. is condemned by the great majority of Christians; but the moral theologian must be prepared to help any individual Christians who are faced by conscientious doubt in the face of this problem. What course of action is to be recommended to such a doubter? First, he should be reminded that A.I.D. is at present illegal in this country and likely to continue to be so in the foreseeable future. Indeed, no state or country has so far given it legal recognition. For many persons this will settle the question: for it is a serious offence to break the civil law deliberately in a grave matter except under the compulsion of conscience. In other words, the couple would have to feel morally bound to resort to A.I.D. in order to

[1] H. Glanville Williams: *The Sanctity of Human Life and the Criminal Law* (1958), p. 112.

justify it. Could they so feel, knowing that it necessarily involves perjury? Even Dean Matthews, who is unwilling to condemn A.I.D. as such, says that he would advise any couple to have nothing to do with it while the law remains as it is.

Leaving the legal aspect of the question aside, however, the doubting couple must face the question as to whether A.I.D. is adultery or in its nature adulterous. The preponderating weight of legal and theological opinion undoubtedly holds that it is. If so, for a Christian, this ends the matter. If, however, the couple persuade themselves that it is not, on the ground that an act of adultery must involve congress, or attempted congress, of the sex organs, they have next to face the question of the deception which A.I.D. involves and the grave psychological risks which it incurs.

If the doubting couple had, in their own minds, surmounted all the foregoing difficulties, it would then be possible for them finally to come to a decision by invoking the principle of double effect. The good effect which is intended is the deliverance from barrenness and the increase of the family; the ill-effect is the deception involved and its possible harmful psychological consequences. Consequently, this action, with its double effect, is legitimised by its good intention, and may be rightly performed, always assuming that the previous difficulties are validly surmounted. It is certainly a large assumption.

We turn to Euthanasia. This may be defined as the deliberate taking of human life for a beneficent purpose. It is commonly said to exist in two forms: (a) compulsory; (b) voluntary. The former is condemned by all Christian moral theologians on the ground that it is a violation of the sacred rights of human personality, and is, in fact, a species of murder, even if performed, as (for example) in Nazi Germany, for the supposed good of the

State. This type of euthanasia, therefore, does not demand any further attention here. The question of voluntary euthanasia, however, is an entirely different matter, and one on which Christian moralists hold different opinions.

Traditionally, voluntary euthanasia has been condemned not, as is sometimes wrongly affirmed, because Christian theology holds that human life has absolute value, but chiefly because man possesses his life on trust from his Creator, to whom alone the issues of life and death belong. It is for the same reason that suicide is condemned.[1]

A good many Christians today, however, do not regard this argument as convincing for several reasons.

In the first place, it is pointed out that modern medical science is making it extremely hard, in some cases, to decide what 'killing' a patient really means, or to say whether, in a given instance, he is 'alive' or 'dead'. For example, artificial methods of breathing or assisting the function of the heart may 'keep a person alive' temporarily. But this raises the question how far is the physician morally bound to continue these methods, and when is he entitled to say that he has tried long enough.[2] That, in a given case, he *is* morally entitled to say this would be generally agreed. Is not this a form of 'euthanasia' it is argued?

Secondly, it is generally agreed, even by opponents of euthanasia, that it is legitimate to ease the pain of a dying patient who is suffering from an alleged incurable disease at the risk of shortening his life. Thus Roman Catholic moral theology accepts this, dealing with this problem by means of the principle of double effect. It is argued that it is the relief of pain which is intended, the shortening of life being regarded here as a subordinate

---

[1] Aquinas: *Summa Theologica*, IIa IIae Q.64, a.5.
[2] See *Decisions about Life and Death* (Church Information Office, 1963).

effect which is not intended. But advocates of euthanasia ask, what is the moral difference between this and what is understood by voluntary euthanasia?

Those who uphold the traditional view, on the other hand, will maintain that there *is* a difference and that the vast majority of physicians know what that difference is. The good doctor is aware of the distinction between prolonging life and prolonging the act of dying.[1] Furthermore, the traditionalist is entitled to point to a consideration which advocates of the legalising of voluntary euthanasia usually fail to take into account. This is the added stress and strain which would be put upon a patient in the grip of a supposedly incurable and painful disease if he knew that the law had given to him the power to ask his doctor to end his life. To have to make such a decision might well be more distressing to him even than his physical symptoms. There is surely great force in the argument that the present law, in its working, is in fact more merciful than would be the law as amended by the voluntary euthanasia society.

Nor is this all. Those who would legalise euthanasia are sometimes inclined to forget that death, and even a painful death, is not the worst that can befall a person. Most important of all here is what is called 'a holy death' *i.e.* a death in which the soul is brought into closer union with God. Legalised euthanasia would almost certainly diminish greatly the likelihood of this.

What, then, is the position of the Christian faced almost certainly by a long-drawn-out and painful death? Is he morally justified in pressing his doctor to give him release? As everybody knows, this is a situation which not infrequently arises; and nobody would wish too harshly to condemn such a patient. Yet the fact remains that in Christian moral theology it would be hard to acquit him

---

[1] Lord Horder in House of Lords debate (5th S.), 103:490 (1936). Quoted by N. St. John Stevas, *Life, Death and the Law*, p. 276.

of sin if he did this. It is significant that Dean Inge, who was himself in favour of legalising euthanasia, found himself confessing that if he were faced by a slow and painful death he hoped that he would be given the grace of God to hang on to the end.

Closely connected with the question of euthanasia is that of suicide; indeed, euthanasia, as it is advocated by the Voluntary Euthanasia Society, is a form of suicide. In the Christian tradition suicide has been universally condemned; and it was S. Augustine who, in this as in other matters, first formulated the traditional doctrine,[1] which was fully systematised by Aquinas. According to the latter, suicide is sinful for three reasons, given in an ascending order of heinousness. First, suicide is an offence against oneself, being a contravention of the natural law of self-preservation which exists in every normal person. Secondly, it is an offence against the community to which the individual belongs, since it deprives it of one of its members. Thirdly, it is an offence against God, in whose hands, as Creator, alone belong the issues of life and death. Hence the command 'Thou shalt not kill'.[2] Two of these three objections became firmly embedded in English Law. So we read in Black-stone's Commentaries: 'The law of England wisely and religiously considers that no man hath a power to destroy life, but by commission from God, the author of it: and, as the suicide is guilty of a double offence; one spiritual in invading the prerogative of the Almighty, and rushing into his immediate presence uncalled for; the other temporal, against the king, who hath an interest in the preservation of all his subjects; the law has there-fore ranked this among the highest crimes, making it a peculiar species of felony committed on oneself.'[3]

The moral theologian, of course, is not, as such,

---

[1] *On the City of God, Book I*, Chap. 20ff.   [2] *Summa Theologica*, IIa IIae Q.64, a.5.
[3] *Op. cit.*, iv, 189, (1775).

concerned directly with the question, recently much canvassed, as to whether or not suicide should be regarded as a crime, but probably the majority of Christians will be glad that this is no longer the case according to the law of England, although aiding and abetting it still is. During the present century it is noticeable that there has been a steady diminution in the strength of the feeling against suicide. The harsh, not to say barbarous, customs which marked the treatment of the body of a suicide and of his possessions a hundred years ago no longer have general approval. This change of atmosphere is doubtless part of the effect of the growth of humanitarianism. But it is also in part most certainly due to the influence of post-Freudian psychology, which has led to the acceptance in law of the principle of diminished responsibility, which we have discussed in an earlier chapter. This means that today the practical difficulty of assessing the degree of responsibility which attaches to any particular act of suicide is widely recognised, and this means that people are increasingly unwilling to pass severe judgement on these unhappy persons. But the Christian has to be careful not to allow his judgement to be clouded on the essential issue which is that deliberate suicide is still to be regarded as a grave sin. This, of course, would not apply to such a famous case as that of the 'gallant gentleman', Captain Oates; for this was clearly an instance of what moral theology calls 'the double effect'. The primary intention of that brave and selfless man was not to commit suicide but to try to preserve the lives of his companions; the suicide was only a by-effect. The reason for the condemnation of suicide has been very well expounded by the authors of *Ought Suicide to be a Crime?* and we cannot do better than to quote what they have written. 'For the Christian, death is something which belongs to our very nature as "fallen man". Whether or not it could be legitimately argued that we inherit some kind of primordial guilt, it is at least true that by our origin, by our very status as human beings, death is inevitable. It comes to all, saint and sinner alike. Death, in short, belongs to us as sharers in a common, unredeemed humanity. It is, indeed, our "last enemy" (1 Cor. 15.26)— the final feature of our earthly existence in which we have to prove that "we are more than conquerors through him that loved us" (Romans 8.37). Whether he lives or dies the Christian is the Lord's (Romans 14.8) and must show himself so to be. The Christian therefore accepts death as that signal occasion when he is finally to prove the love and power of God in Christ. He sees death as the last and crucial occasion for the testing of his faith, where victory is to be won in Christ and his redemption fulfilled.[1] The death of the suicide is a denial of all this, and that is why, from the Christian point of view, it must always be wrong, although in any individual case, God is the judge and not man; but this is true of all our actions and not only of the act of suicide. This elementary fact seems to be too often overlooked in discussions on this subject.

We now come to a moral problem which, although as old as mankind, has in modern times assumed alarming proportions, and that is gambling. The sum of money involved in gambling in this country has now assumed astronomical proportions, according to the latest figures.

No Christian would deny that here is a colossal social evil which has exceeded all bounds, owing to its commercialisation. Enormous prizes are now offered to those who are ready to participate in football pools and other forms of organised commercial gambling. Moreover, it is said that nearly a quarter of a million persons are now engaged in this country in servicing this 'industry' which is not only socially harmful but economically

[1] *Op. cit.*, p. 28.

useless—persons who might otherwise be engaged in some form of productive enterprise. Moreover, in the case of those who are occupied in productive work many thousands of working hours are lost annually owing to the distractions of betting on horse-racing on days when there is a big race. William Temple once said that gambling is the most prolific source of evil which could be named, leading to idleness, irresponsibility, covetousness and other evils; and many would agree with him. All this raises no problem for the moral theologian. Gambling organised in this way is sinful and a great social evil. But unfortunately he cannot allow the problem to rest there. He is obliged to face the awkward question: Is gambling in any and every form *per se* wrong?

Before trying to answer this question it is essential to decide upon a definition of gambling; for the word is apt to be used very loosely and this leads to confused and slovenly thinking, so that people literally do not know what they are talking about. Thus we hear people say that all life is a gamble or that the activities of the Stock Exchange are a form of gambling, and even that all forms of insurance are a gamble. Such talk is misleading and confusing. None of these activities are, properly speaking, to be reckoned as gambling, merely because they are concerned with risks.

Let us, therefore, define gambling as follows: 'The gambling contract is an agreement between two parties whereby the transfer of something of value from one to the other is made dependent on an uncertain event (which before the agreement was made did not constitute a risk to either party) in such a way that one party will gain and the other will lose'.[1]

Certain points in this definition should be noted. First, gambling involves a contract between two parties.

[1] *Gambling: An Ethical Discussion* (Church Information Office, 1950), p. 16.

This contract is an agreement to appeal to a risk which would not otherwise involve the parties. Secondly, the contract involves the transfer of some object of value—usually money—from the one party to the other, so that the loss of the former is balanced by the gain of the latter. This definition clearly covers, without exception, every wager and betting contract, every gaming contract and every lottery. It is equally clear that it does not apply to insurance contracts or to dealings on the Stock Exchange, for every gain there involves at least two contracts, one for buying and one for selling. Speculation on a big scale is, of course, possible on the Stock Exchange and it is doubtless most harmful in its effects, but it is not, in strictness, to be classed as gambling.

Having clearly defined, therefore, what is meant—or ought to be meant—by the word 'gambling', we have next to enquire whether it is necessarily and *per se* wrong, or whether, in certain circumstances it is permissible. There are some who would argue that the former is the case, and that it is never lawful to indulge in the mildest form of gambling—for instance to bet a friend a shilling that Oxford will win the next boat race. Yet, in fact, it is extremely difficult to maintain this position, and, generally speaking, moral theology asserts that gambling is not inherently wrong: accordingly the Church has never condemned gambling *per se*. It involves, as we have seen a deliberate appeal to chance, and it has sometimes been argued that such an appeal is in itself wrong. Yet it is not easy to understand why it should be. There are indeed many occasions in life when it is obviously wrong to take a chance, as, for instance in all serious matters—matters of life and death, as we say, or of critical importance. Yet there are equally clearly other occasions when it seems obvious that there is no harm in doing this. For instance, in playing games, in order to decide who is to have the choice of which goal to defend first, in football, or which team is to bat first in cricket, the only practicable way is to agree to decide by an appeal to chance. It is, therefore, not easy to see why an appeal to chance should not also be made just for the fun of the thing by means of a betting contract. 'Just for the fun of the thing': here is the moral justification for gambling. It is a form of entertainment, and, if it costs something, like other forms of entertainment, why should it on that account be condemned? If, however, gambling is to be approved, moral theology insists that certain stringent conditions must be observed. Because these conditions are, in the vast majority of cases, not observed, we must not on that account condemn gambling out of hand. It has been rightly said that there are quite enough varieties of sin in the world without needlessly adding to their number. The Report of the Social and Industrial Commission which has been already quoted sums up the situation concisely when it says: 'Circumstances may make gambling unjust, but the contract is not unjust in itself.'[1] Perhaps this statement would have been better expressed if it had suggested that circumstances *usually* make gambling unjust; for as we shall see, the conditions in which it is lawful are stringent and commonly ignored.

According to moral theology, in order that the gambling contract may be lawful, the four following conditions must be observed:

(*a*) the contract must be concerned with an event which is equally and genuinely uncertain for both parties; otherwise it would be unjust. (For example, it would be wrong for a party to bet on a certain horse not winning a race, if it was known to that party that the horse in question was to be doped.)

(*b*) The contracting parties must have the free disposal[2] of the money involved in the stakes and be in a position to risk the loss of it without defaulting on any duties. Thus it is wrong to

---

[1] *Op. cit.*, p. 25.
[2] See *e.g.* Prümmer: *Manuale Theologiae Moralis*, Vol. 2, p. 263.

gamble with other people's money or with money which is required for household expenses.

(c) The contract must be such as not to involve either of the parties in what is called by moral theologians 'co-operation in sin'. That is to say, it is not enough for gambler A to be able to say that he can legitimately afford the stake involved as entertainment money, which he is spending 'for the fun of the thing'. He must also be assured that he is not involved by his gamble with any other person B who cannot afford to lose the stake, as he can. This is a very stringent condition indeed. It will be seen that it rules out all forms of commercialised gambling, and most forms of organised gambling, for obviously nobody who takes part in these can be in a position to know that all the other parties involved are in a position to lose their stakes without defaulting on any duties. If the stakes are very low indeed—like a sixpenny raffle ticket—this can be assumed. But when the stakes are of any substance the gamble cannot be entered into without the danger of 'co-operating in sin'. The observance of this condition excludes all organised betting and lotteries of every kind except those which involve only very low stakes indeed.

(d) The primary motive of entering into the gambling contract must be 'the fun of the thing' and not the winning of money;[1] for, as we have seen, gambling is lawful only for its amusement value.

It will be clear from what has been said that these conditions rule out the greater part of gambling as it is practised today; and there are some people who argue, in consequence, that it is far wiser and better to condemn gambling root and branch than to attempt vainly to hedge it about with restrictions which few will in practice ever observe. The answer to this must be to say that truth is all important and that if, in fact, gambling in certain forms *is* harmless it is the duty of the Christian moralist fearlessly to say this, at whatever cost. We must not 'tell lies for God'.

The matter must ultimately be faced by the conscience of each individual Christian. He may well decide

[1] Prümmer, *Op. cit.*, Vol. 2, p. 264.

that taking everything into account it is his duty as a Christian to have nothing to do with it. If so, nobody can condemn him: for clearly nobody can have a duty to gamble, unless, indeed, one should on occasion feel impelled to do so in the interests of charity as, for example, when one is invited to make a fourth at bridge, when stakes are involved, otherwise the game would be spoiled. On the other hand, those who do not feel bound in conscience to follow the strictest line and avoid gambling in every shape or form have, as Christians, to be very careful indeed how they deal with this question; for gambling is, as we have seen, morally dangerous. They will have to scrutinise every gambling proposition which comes before them before they accept it.

In this connexion there is one form of gambling which calls for special mention because it concerns a good many Christians, and that is the buying of Premium Bonds. What has the moral theologian to say about these? It is sometimes argued that there is no gambling here, for all parties will have their stakes returned to them in full, whenever they wish, and, in any case, they will automatically be returned in full at their death. Therefore (it is said) there is no risk of the contracting parties losing anything, consequently it is not a gambling contract. This, however, is not so, as Professor Thomas Wood has pointed out.[1] There *is* a risk of loss involved, and that is the loss of the interest on the sum invested in the Bonds. Thus a person who holds £100 worth of those Bonds and who over a period of five years receives no prize, loses, at 5 per cent, £25: a person with a large holding in such circumstances would lose a good deal more. It cannot, therefore, be argued that there is no risk involved, and it is possible, even if unlikely, that some holders of the Bonds are risking more than they can afford to lose, so that the possessor of any of these Bonds is in fact involved

[1] T. Wood: *Some Moral Problems* (1961), p. 92.

in the possibility of being a co-operator in sin, even if the possibility is small. It is small because any Bond owner can get back the whole of his stake at any time if his essential obligations are in jeopardy.

Is the moral theologian obliged to say, therefore, that no Christian can enter into the Premium Bonds contract without sin? Before finally reaching this conclusion there is one other consideration of which account must be taken. We have seen that in the case of Premium Bonds the risk of loss concerns not the capital invested but the interest only. It is, however, well known that in the Church there is a long-standing tradition that money is 'barren' and, in consequence, rates of interest have been suspect and, when they are high, condemned. If, therefore, a holder of Premium Bonds is content to take the risk involved in forgoing the interest on his money for an indefinite period, in the hope of receiving in the end a higher rate of interest is he to be condemned? The point is a nice one, and perhaps leads to the conclusion that it would be overscrupulous to condemn the gambling involved in holding Premium Bonds, although it must be conceded that the entertainment value of scanning the monthly results of the draw in the newspapers is not high. Each man must be fully persuaded in his own mind, as S. Paul would say.

We turn finally to the problem of the Christian attitude to war. Like most of the questions which we have been discussing this has been greatly changed by modern scientific inventions and developments. The problem resolves itself into two closely related questions: (1) Is it permissible for a country to make war and for Christians to take part in it? (2) What restrictions are required to make a war legitimate, it being generally agreed by Christians that *some* restrictions are required?

The traditional answer to the first question is clearly and concisely expressed in Article 37 of the Thirty-Nine

H

Articles, in the Latin version, which runs: *Christianis licet ex mandato magistratus, arma portare et iusta bella administrare.* Three points are to be noted in this statement. (1) It is lawful for Christians to fight; not, it is the duty of Christians to fight. In other words, a place is left for the conscientious objector, as English law has always recognised, and there have always been Christians who have been pacifists. The Christian Church, however, has never been pacifist. (2) The war must be an act of State, not a rebellion by unconstituted authority. (3) It must be a 'just' war. Here the English version of the Article fails badly, *'iusta bella administrare'* in the Latin being rendered 'serve in the wars', the vital word *'iusta'* being completely ignored.

This brings us to the second of the two questions proposed at the beginning. What restrictions are required to make a war 'just'? The first attempt to face this question seriously was made by S. Augustine of Hippo who laid the foundation of the moral theology of war. The basis of his position is that a war must have a just cause and a right intention: otherwise, he says: *'quid aliud quam grande latrocinium?'*[1] Its objective must be the restoration of peace.[2] He recognised that the just are not always victorious, arguing that war is often God's way of punishing the wicked and chastising the just.

Aquinas finally systematised S. Augustine's teaching, developing it in connexion with the doctrine of natural law. S. Paul's teaching in Romans 13.4 was most influential here: 'He (*sc.* the ruler) is a minister of God to thee for good . . . for he beareth not the sword in vain.' This teaching became the foundation of the doctrine of international law as expressed in the great work of Grotius, *De Jure Belli et Pacis.* Grotius argues that 'the right of self-defence arises from the natural right of self-protection, not from the injustice or fault of another.

---

[1] *On the City of God*, Book IV, Chap. 7.   [2] *Ibid.*, Book XIX, Chap. 11.

Therefore this right of self-protection is not taken away even if the aggressor be blameless'.[1] And this, he argues, applies to states also.

Thus was formed the traditional Christian teaching concerning war, and this found its way into Anglican moral theology. So Jeremy Taylor (for example) says: 'Force is the defensative of all laws; and when all laws are injured, there can be no way to reduce men to reason, but by making them feel the evils of unreasonableness. If this were not so, commonwealths were in a worse state of affairs than single persons: for princes are to defend each single person; and the laws are to secure them; but if the laws themselves be not defended, no single person can be; and if they could much rather should all. Whatsoever is absolutely necessary is certainly lawful.'[2] But he adds later: 'They must keep themselves within the limits of a just defence.' The 'innocent' must not be destroyed with the guilty, 'the peaceable countryman with the fighting soldier'.[3] Here we see a reference to the distinction drawn by the medieval lawyers between *nocentes* and *innocentes*, *i.e.* those *directly* concerned in sustaining the war effort and those not. This is a much more satisfactory distinction than the modern distinction between 'combatants' and 'noncombatants'.

We have now to face the vital question as to how far the foregoing traditional principles are applicable to our present age of (at least) potential nuclear warfare. There are some Christians who hold that they are not applicable at all. The invention of nuclear weapons which are *per se* totally indiscriminate over a huge area have made them meaningless. Nuclear war (they argue) being total war makes it impossible to observe any of the traditional limitations or restrictions.

[1] *Ibid.*, Book II, Chap. 1.   [2] *Ductor Dubitantium*, Book II, Chap. II, Rule 7.
[3] *Ibid.*

What, then, must be the Christian attitude to war and to the manufacture and testing of nuclear weapons? Here there is a deep cleavage of opinion. On the one side are those who argue that Christians cannot tolerate these weapons and who press for disarmament—even unilateral disarmament—at whatever risk. The only Christian course to take (they say) is to have nothing whatever to do with them. 'The nuclear deterrent enters a dimension of violence so flatly contrary to the Christian faith that there is no course open to the Christian other than to renounce these intrinsically evil weapons. Not until the step of renunciation has been taken will Christians feel themselves in a position to hear what God is saying to them.'[1] Undoubtedly many Christians think in this way, but not all, probably not the majority. On the other side stand those who believe that it is the duty of the State to hold 'the nuclear deterrent' as the only hope of preventing war. It seems to be generally agreed that it is the existence of this deterrent which alone has so far prevented a third world war. If the non-Communist countries were to throw this away, it would lead to the enslavement of the whole world to the domination of Communism, which professedly believes in the primacy of force.

There is a further division among those who favour the holding of nuclear weapons as a deterrent. Some maintain that it is legitimate to hold nuclear weapons as a deterrent, but only with the secret mental reservation never to use them. Others, on the contrary, believe that in the last resort these terrible weapons could legitimately be used. This view was expressed by the Anglican Commission appointed by the two English Archbishops in 1945, which reported three years later. They say in their report, which was issued with only one dissentient voice: 'On the assumption that today the possession of

[1] *The British Nuclear Deterrent* (S.C.M. Press, 1963), p. 27.

atomic weapons is genuinely necessary for national self-preservation, a government, which is responsible for the safety of the community committed to its charge, is entitled to manufacture them and hold them in readiness. The Commission believes, moreover, that in certain circumstances defensive "necessity" might justify their use against an unscrupulous aggressor."[1]

Those who take this view today are appealing to the principle of choosing the lesser evil. They argue that even to engage in a nuclear war would be a lesser evil than to allow the world to be subjected *for ever* to Communist domination; for it would be for ever. Obviously no power could possibly arise which would be able to overthrow the victor in a nuclear world war, since he would have sole control of nuclear weapons.

Turning to the problem of the individual Christian concerning war, nuclear warfare really simplifies his difficulty; for *ex hypothesi* a nuclear war would not drag on. Everybody would be involved from the first. There would be no problem of enlistment as in the two world wars.

If, however, a war breaks out which is waged only with conventional weapons, as, for example, is the case with the Vietnam war, the problem remains unchanged. He has to obey his conscience in deciding whether it is his duty to enlist or to proclaim himself a conscientious objector. In coming to his decision he will have to settle in his own mind which is the lesser of two evils, to fight for his country in a 'just' war or not to fight.

[1] *The Church and the Atom:* A Study of the Moral and Theological Aspects of Peace and War (1948), p. 111.

5

Sin and Imperfection

MORAL THEOLOGY presupposes the fact of sin. The moral theologian, as such, is not obliged to try to prove its existence; rather is it his task to examine its nature, to classify the various types of sin, and to assist the priest and the pastor in dealing with it. Nevertheless, since, as Bishop Barry has recently remarked, 'there is probably no word that is less acceptable to the "modern" mind than the word sin',[1] and, as modern books on ethics ignore its existence entirely, something may usefully be said here about the connexion between sin and morality. If the moral theologian is to justify himself in the eyes of the philosopher, at least, he has to show that ethics, rightly understood, necessarily involves the concept of sin, which (he holds) cannot be explained away as a fad of the theologian.

The fact is that any attempt to explain away the idea of sin as the equivalent of mere error, or failure in evolutionary adjustment fails entirely to do justice to the deliverances of the moral consciousness. There is, indeed, as Socrates insisted, an element of deception in all wrong doing. Evil is made to appear good. No sane person deliberately does evil because it is evil. If Richard III says, 'I am determined to prove a villain',[2] that is only because it appears to him as something worth doing

---

[1] F. R. Barry: *Christian Ethics and Secular Society* (1966), p. 67.
[2] Shakespeare, *Richard the Third*, Act i, Scene i.

and to that extent good. Archbishop Temple was surely right when he wrote: 'That any man can choose evil, knowing it to be evil *for him*, is to me quite incredible. He may say, under an impulse of defiance, "Evil, be thou my good"; but his pursuit of it is then due to the fact that he has adopted it as his good and not because it is evil. To desire evil strictly for its own sake is impossible.'[1] It is, of course, possible to know the better, and choose the worse: *Video meliora proboque deteriora sequor*. But at the moment of choice the worse appears to be good, otherwise it would never be chosen.

Nevertheless, this element of deception in wrong doing is not the whole story. Although we may be deceived by sin, at the same time we do not feel that this exonerates us. We feel that we are, nevertheless, to blame. We ought not to have been deceived, and in our hearts we know that if we had been better men or women we should not have been deceived. This, as Professor A. E. Taylor pointed out, is not 'an illusion bred of antecedent theological prepossession'. 'It is not . . . theology which has contaminated ethics with the notion of *sin*; it is morality which has brought the notion into theology.'[2] He goes on to say: 'In more ways than one, our human expression of wrong doing and guilt is so singularly unlike anything that we can detect in the pre-human world that we are bound to treat it as something *sui generis* and *human* not generically animal.'[3] Nor, it must be said, can it be fully accounted for in terms of merely human relationships.

That is why the Freudian attempt to explain away conscience by reducing it to the 'super-ego' fails to do justice to the facts. It is easy to show that there are elements in our sense of wrong doing which cannot be so explained. First, let us notice the experience which was

---

[1] W. Temple: *Nature, Man and God* (1934), p. 362.
[2] A. E. Taylor: *The Faith of a Moralist* (1930), I, p. 169.
[3] *Ibid.*, p. 170.

described by the ancient Greeks as *hubris*. According to this way of thinking there is an attitude of mind which leads to conduct which is so disgraceful that it must in the end lead to disaster. It is conduct of such a kind that no right-minded person could contemplate it. Such, for example, is the practice of using poisoned arrows. The moral condemnation of this, as Gilbert Murray has pointed out, is not derived from experience. It is not because, in practice, the use of poisoned arrows always leads directly to retribution. It is because we 'feel in our bones' that this is something too horrible to be tolerated. This belief, and other similar beliefs, cannot be accounted for as being the judgement of the super-ego based on experience. It can only be understood as the shadow of the eternal cast upon the temporal. In other words, moral evil is sin. There are some actions which are so horrible to us that they cry to high heaven for retribution.

A second type of moral experience which reveals very clearly the shadow of the eternal on the temporal is our attitude to wrong done in the past. Here we find that we are unable just to leave the evil past behind us and forget about it, which might appear the reasonable thing to do. It is not possible merely to 'let bygones be bygones' when matters of grave conscience are concerned, as is possible in merely human relationships. We cannot just 'forget it'. There are times when we are unable to forgive ourselves even if others are ready to forgive. That is because our offence, if it is a grave offence, is something which transcends the time process. Nothing that *we* can do can put things right.

> Could my tears for ever flow
> Could my zeal no respite know
> All for sin cannot atone.

These familiar words occur in a Christian setting,

where the belief is expressed that in Christ atonement, the wiping out of the past, *is* possible. But the point to notice here is that this moral experience clearly shows that, apart from what Christianity or any other religion may teach, the evil past cannot just be treated as if it had never been; and no human power can put this right. The only way in which that can happen, the only way in which the evil past can be really forgotten is if we can come to see that it has been transmuted into a greater good.[1] We shall return to this point later, when we come to think of forgiveness. Here it is enough to see it as another example of the shadow of the eternal upon the temporal, indicating that the idea of sin is inherent in moral experience. No account of what morality is can be regarded as adequate, if it ignores this. In short, wrong doing is, in the last analysis, what the moral theologian calls sin. It is something done 'against heaven',[2] and not merely against the super-ego.

Assuming, then, the fact of sin as disobedience to God, the moral theologian proceeds to analyse the different forms which sin can take. In this analysis there are four primary distinctions to be taken into account.

(*a*) Between Actual and Original Sin.
(*b*) Between Actual and Habitual Sin.
(*c*) Between Mortal and Venial Sin.
(*d*) Between Formal and Material Sin.

We now proceed to a discussion of these different kinds of sin.

(a) *Actual and Original Sin*
This distinction is fundamental to Christian theology, although from the days of Pelagius in the fifth century it has been denied or, more often, ignored. What is the basis of this distinction? It is the familiar fact that *all*

---

[1] Cf. Dante, *Paradiso*, ix, 103–6.   [2] S. Luke 15.21.

men are from the hour of their birth completely self-centred, and that the process of being delivered from that selfishness is long and painful. In other words, this means 'that every human being has in one respect or another a bias or tendency to evil' and this is 'not a mysterious doctrine but (for) an evident and vitally important fact'. So wrote Archbishop William Temple in his Gifford Lectures;[1] and no modern theologian has more clearly understood the nature of that fact than he.

This self-centred bias in mankind, Temple pointed out, is quite different from the self-centredness of an unself-conscious animal. By contrast it is a deliberate selfishness whereby the individual chooses which ends to pursue in his own supposed interests. Consequently it cannot be adequately explained as an evolutionary hang-over from the ape and the tiger. It does not reside in the instinctive drives and appetites, although these can be troublesome enough, as Temple says. It resides in the whole self-conscious personality which is self-centred instead of being God-centred—egoistic instead of being altruistic. This can easily be seen in the human infant which flies into a passion if its imperious desires are not satisfied and satisfied at once. This did not escape that acute observer, S. Augustine, when he wrote: 'Who can tell me the sin of my infancy? For none is clean from sin in Thy sight, not even the infant whose life upon earth is but one day long. Who can tell me? Shall I not reply, Any tiny little creature in whom I see what I cannot recollect? How then did I sin? Was it that I craved with tears for the breast? For if I were now to crave so greedily, not for the breast but for dainties suited to my years, most justly should I be ridiculed and blamed. Even then, therefore, I deserved blame; but custom and reason saved me from blame, because I could not understand it. For we root out and cast away these childish ways as we

[1] W. Temple: *Nature, Man and God* (1934), pp. 363, 364.

grow. Yet I never saw anyone who tried to mend by casting away what he knew to be good. Or may we say that for the time it was good to beg with tears what could only hurt if given, to fly into a passion because freemen, elders, parents would not humour a whim, because the wise would not run at our beck and call, to try to strike and hurt with all our might because our sovereign will was not obeyed, tho' it could not be obeyed except to our harm? If so, the innocence of infancy depends on the weakness of its limbs, not on its character. I know, because I have seen jealousy in a babe. It could not speak, yet it eyed its twin with pale cheeks and look of hate.'[1]

It is this inherited bias which makes the early training of the human infant so difficult a matter, and that is why the behaviour of the infant cannot be rightly understood by comparing it with the behaviour of Pavlov's dogs, as, for example, Dr. Frank Lake suggests in his *Clinical Theology*.[2] Indeed, it is a serious weakness in that book that in setting forth the psychological difficulties of the human infant in the first year after birth he takes no account of this inherited bias of original sin which from the very first bedevils human relationships.

The human infant emerges from the womb utterly weak and defenceless, entirely dependent on its mother or mother surrogate not for weeks or days, like other species, but for years. Consequently the human mother has the delicate and difficult task of sustaining the child both physically and mentally, giving it just the right amount of support until it gradually attains first to full self-consciousness and then to independence. If too much 'mothering' is given to the child, its inherited egocentricity is fostered and you have the pampered and 'spoiled' child. If too little, you have the fear-ridden and

---

[1] *Confessions*, Book I, Chap. 7 (Bigg's translation), pp. 43 and 44.
[2] F. Lake: *Clinical Theology* (1966), pp. 610 ff.

neglected child. But the point whch has to be noticed here is that the course of this development which would otherwise have been smooth and easy is made difficult, sometimes acutely difficult, by this inherited egocentric bias which we call original sin. The tantrums which result are by no means 'biological necessities', as, for example, F. R. Tennant[1] argued; they are, as we have seen, without parallel in the sub-human species. What is more, this evil bias in man is never completely eradicated. That is why sin dogs his footsteps from the cradle to the grave.

(b) *Actual and Habitual Sin*

We pass to a consideration of the distinction between actual sin and habitual sin which is made in moral theology. Habitual sin is not, as a recent Anglican writer[2] has said, 'a sin which has come to be a habit'. It is something entirely different; it is the effect or stain (*macula*)[3] of sin in the soul, that loss of sanctifying grace which follows upon mortal sin. When we deliberately do something wrong, it is not something over and done with, as we say. Unfortunately it leaves behind it abiding consequences—not only the chain but also the stain of sin. This stain remains until it is removed by God's forgiveness. In Roman Catholic moral theology this normally means by the sacrament of penance; but in all moral theology it means when it is blotted out by God's forgiveness, following upon repentance. Even in Roman Catholic moral theology, if the contrition is perfect, absolution is not necessary. According to Anglican moral theology, it is left to the individual conscience to decide[4] in any given case whether absolution is required. The

---

[1] F. R. Tennant: *The Origin and Propagation of Sin*, p. 100.
[2] H. M. Waddams: *A New Introduction to Moral Theology* (1964), p. 232.
[3] Aquinas, *Summa Theologica*, Ia IIa Q.85, a.1 and Q.86, a.1.
[4] *Book of Common Prayer*, Office for the Visitation of the Sick.

essential point is that the stain of sin is a terrible reality with which we have to reckon. Such is habitual sin.

There can be no doubt that the Anglican position in this matter of contrition and repentance is securely founded in early Christian theology. Bishop Kirk wrote: 'In the primitive period—in the days, for example, of Hermas, Clement and Polycarp—little stress was laid upon absolution, much upon the efficacy of true penitence ("perfect contrition" as it came later to be called) to win complete forgiveness from God. The instances of Lazarus who was called to life again *before* the disciples "unbound" him, and of the lepers who were healed before "they showed themselves to the priests", were for long interpreted to mean that divine forgiveness *preceded* official readmission to communion by the Church. So strongly was it felt that perfect contrition won complete forgiveness without any intermediate ecclesiastical action, that even the most convinced churchmen—Jerome, Augustine, Gregory the Great and Anselm—can be quoted as supporters of the position. Importance was attached, of course, to the presence and co-operation of the bishop or priest. But different views were held as to his function. The form of absolution until the twelfth century was precatory and not declaratory'.[1] But this does not imply, as Kirk proceeds to point out, that this means that absolution merely declares the fact of forgiveness already bestowed. He rightly adds, in favour of the later position, that although it remains true that 'perfect contrition' automatically wins forgiveness 'a truer psychology saw how rare such "perfect contrition" must be'. The true doctrine of absolution must, therefore, surely be that it makes good the deficiencies of the contrition of the penitent by the merits of our Lord Jesus Christ,[2] who, as R. C. Moberly so powerfully argued, is

---

[1] K. E. Kirk: *The Vision of God* (1932), pp. 287 and 288.
[2] See my *Moral Theology in the Modern World* (1964), pp. 95ff.

the only perfect penitent because (paradoxically) he alone is without sin. The penitent Christian, therefore, will not despise what the Prayer Book calls 'the benefit of absolution'. Indeed, we should expect to find that the more truly penitent he is the more will he acknowledge and bewail his lack of contrition; and this is exactly what we do find. Broadly speaking, but only broadly speaking, it is the more devout and not the less devout who feel the need of the benefit of absolution in the Anglican Church, where no member of the Church is under any external compulsion in this matter.

(c) *Mortal and Venial Sin*

We now come to a distinction which has led to much controversy, which still has not died down, and that is the distinction between mortal and venial sin. Some Anglican moral theologians, both in the past and in the present, would repudiate this distinction, although it is rooted in the Scriptures of both the Old and the New Testaments. First, it is rooted in the Old Testament—a fact which has been almost universally ignored—in the distinction between sins committed 'with a high hand', for which the sacrificial system did not avail, and other offences called *Shegagoth*.[1] The penalty for the former was expulsion from the covenant relationship. *Shegagoth* included 'all sins done not in a spirit of rebellion against the law or ordinance of Jehovah—sins committed through human imperfection, or human ignorance or human passion; sins done when the mind was directed to some end connected with human weakness or selfishness, but not formally opposed to the authority of the lawgiver. The distinction was thus primarily a distinction in regard to the state of mind of the transgressor'.[2] It is, therefore, not surprising that we find this distinction

---

[1] Numbers 15.22–31.
[2] A. B. Davidson: *Old Testament Theology* (1904), p. 315.

carried on into the New Testament, when it appears unequivocally in the First Epistle of S. John as 'sin unto death' and 'sin not unto death' (1 John 5.16 and 17).

These expressions are explicitly rendered in the Revised Standard Version as sin which is 'not mortal' and sin which is 'mortal'. There 'not mortal' is the equivalent of 'venial'. It is most surprising that Jeremy Taylor, in opposing this distinction,[1] makes no reference to this passage, and the same is usually the case with present-day opponents of the distinction. Furthermore, there are other New Testament passages which draw attention to the much greater gravity of some sins than others—*e.g.* S. John 19.11 when Our Lord tells Pilate that those who delivered him into his hands were guilty of 'the greater sin', or S. Mark 3.28–30 and parallels where there is reference to a sin which has no forgiveness. While, of course, it is true to say that even between mortal sins there are differences of degree—*e.g.* rape is more wicked than mutually agreed fornication, and stealing from a church is more wicked than stealing from a neighbour—it is also true that some sins are comparatively slight, if they are sins of frailty. It flies in the face of common sense to deny this fact, which ultimately is the basis of the distinction between 'mortal' and 'venial' sin. As S. Augustine wrote; to assert the parity of sins (as the Stoics did) 'is as if we should say that mice and elephants are equal because they are both animals, or that flies and eagles are equal because they both can fly'.[2]

Thus to deny the existence of minimal sins is to flout common sense, and there can be no doubt that some writers have done this at times. Jeremy Taylor surely did in the passage quoted above: 'It is a less evil that all mankind should be destroyed than that God should be displeased in the least instance that is imaginable.'[3] Still

---

[1] As we shall see, he is not whole-hearted about this.   [2] Epist. 104.4.14.
[3] *Unum Necessarium*, Chap. 3, § 1,

more did Newman so when he wrote: 'The Church holds that it were better for sun and moon to drop from heaven, for the earth to fail, and for all the many millions who are upon it to die of starvation in extremest agony, so far as temporal affliction goes, than that one soul, I will not say should be lost, but should commit one single venial sin, should tell one wilful untruth, though it harmed no one, or steal one poor farthing without excuse.'[1] Dean Inge was surely right when he described this sentence as 'monstrous and absurd'.[2]

The common law of England is wiser than this when it lays it down: *De minimis non curat lex*—a dictum which is founded in Roman law. In its original form it ran: *De minimis non curat Praetor.*

Why, then, has exception been taken to this distinction between mortal and venial sin? There seem to be two main reasons. First, it is said that it encourages moral laxity and leads to the belief that venial sins do not matter. So Jeremy Taylor says, 'To distinguish a whole kind of sins is a certain way to make repentance and amendment of life imperfect and false', and again, 'It is rather a dispensation or leave to commit one sort of them.'[3] So a modern writer has said: 'To divide sins in this way is bound to give the impression that there are some sins which matter and some which do not. No amount of explanation can avoid this impression.'[4]

In the second place, there is the kindred objection that this distinction is bound to lead in the end to an entirely wrong attitude to sin and to contentment with a low moral standard. 'It takes men's attention away from the love of God and focuses it upon the legal requirements of external actions.'[5]

There is, however, a clear and simple answer to these

---

[1] Quoted by W. R. Inge, *Christian Ethics and Modern Problems* (1931), p. 107.
[2] *Ibid.*   [3] *Unum Necessarium*, Chap. 3, § 4.
[4] H. M. Waddams: *A New Introduction to Moral Theology* (1964), p. 100.
[5] *Ibid.*, p. 101.

objections. It is found in the maxim, *abusus non tollit usum;* for no fair-minded person can deny that this distinction has its uses. These are in the main two. First, it is of value in the hands of the priest and pastor. As Kirk has said, 'Everything depends upon the emphasis and the direction in which the distinction is employed. It may help the man who is in little danger of mortal sin to look upwards, making the eradication even of venial sin his final ambition; such a result is evidence that the doctrine has been put to wise and fruitful use. Or it may help him to look downward, and rest complacently on the fact that he is not as other men are; that leads direct to Pharisaism and spiritual stagnation. In any case the doctrine itself is not evil; it is a true statement of fact and nothing more. It takes its usefulness or harmfulness from the livery which from time to time it is caused to wear.'[1] That is well said.

Aquinas states the distinction thus: 'When the soul is so far disordered by sin as to be turned from its last end, which is God, to whom it is united by love, that is mortal sin; but when it is disordered without turning away from God, that is venial sin.' He then proceeds to illustrate this difference by referring to the distinction between two kinds of bodily disease, that which kills and that which only causes illness. For a sin to be mortal it must be sin knowingly and wilfully committed as contrasted with sins due to frailty, which do not come from the heart and the will. More technically expressed, mortal sin requires three conditions: (*a*) Fully conscious knowledge of what is being done. For example, a person half-asleep or intoxicated is not capable of committing a mortal sin: the same would apply to a person acting under duress or violence; (*b*) the agent must fully assent to the action; (*c*) the matter must not be trivial. Thus to steal a halfpenny could not be mortal sin, nor to tell a 'white lie'.

[1] K. E. Kirk: *The Vision of God,* p. 249.

I

In giving spiritual counsel, whether in the confessional or outside it, the priest needs a standard or yardstick to guide him, and here this distinction between mortal and venial sin has proved itself. In the right hands and with the right intention it is of great value. The objections commonly urged against the distinction are no more than objections to its abuse.

There is, however, a second way in which this distinction between mortal and venial sin is of value, and that is in connexion with the scrupulous conscience. The scrupulous person makes mountains out of molehills, and is apt to lose all sense of proportion in passing moral judgement on himself. For such a one to be assured by the priest that he is certainly not guilty of sin unto death or of the unforgivable sin can be an overwhelming relief and spiritual blessing. Only those who have had to deal with scrupulous souls can fully appreciate what this means. We are surely bound to conclude that, although this distinction between mortal and venial sin can be abused easily enough, this is not sufficient reason for discarding it altogether. In the end, even Jeremy Taylor finds himself bound to accept it. He says, in reference to the Roman Catholic teaching on penance: 'But as care is taken that their doctrines do not destroy charity or good life by looseness and indulgence, so care must be taken that ours do not destroy hope and discountenance the endeavours of pious people; for if the smallest sins be so highly punishable, who can hope ever to escape the intolerable state of damnation? And if God can be eternally angry for those things which we account small sins, then no man is a servant or a friend of God; no man is in the estate of the divine favour; for no man is without these sins; for they are such *Quae non possit homo quisquam evitare cavendo*, "which a man, by all his industry, cannot wholly avoid". Now because the Scripture pronounces some persons "just" and "righteous" as David and

Josiah, Zachary and Elizabeth, who yet could not be
pure and innocent from small offences: either these little
things are in their own nature venial, or the godly have
leave to do that which is punished in the ungodly; or
some other way must be found out, how that which is in
its own nature damnable, can stand with the state of
grace; and upon what causes, sins which of themselves are
not so, may come to be venial, that is, more apt and
ready to be pardoned, and in the next disposition to
receive a mercy.'[1]

(d) Formal and Material Sin.

This is a highly important distinction for the moral
theologian; for it draws attention to the difference
between wrongdoing and culpability. The two are not
coterminous. Unfortunately, however, there is some
confusion in the use of these terms. According to
Prümmer: 'Formal sin is the free and culpable transgression of the divine law. Material sin is the transgression
of the divine law through invincible ignorance or through
force which destroys the internal consent'.[2] Some other
moralists, however, omit the crucial word 'invincible'
in this definition, thus making material sin to be any
transgression due to ignorance, even vincible ignorance.
So, for example, Watkin Williams says: '*Formal Sin* is
sin knowingly and freely committed. *Material Sin* is an
act which is objectively sinful, but which is not knowingly
and freely committed.'[3] This definition slurs over the
vital distinction between vincible and invincible ignorance. This seems to be most unfortunate, for the whole
purpose of distinguishing between formal and material
sin is to distinguish between wrongdoing which is
blameworthy and wrongdoing which is not. If, however,
an action proceeds from vincible ignorance (which is

[1] *Op. cit.*, Chap. III, Section 4.40. [2] *Op. cit.*, I, 360.
[3] Watkin Williams: *The Moral Theology of the Sacrament of Penance* (1919), p. 176.

blameworthy) the action must also be blameworthy. Kirk was involved in the same confusion, when he wrote: 'This (*sc.* the distinction between formal and material sin) corresponds, as we have seen, to the distinction we drew between sinful acts and habits deliberately committed or contracted by the sinner with full knowledge of their real character, and those of whose danger he *ought to have* been conscious, but in fact was not. In the latter case the true sin—the real problem to be handled—lies not in the act or habit itself, but in the *culpable* and *vincible* ignorance which caused it.'[1] We shall, therefore, adhere to the position adopted by Prümmer and hold that for sin to be material, as contrasted with formal, the ignorance from which it springs must be invincible. So far as I am aware neither Jeremy Taylor nor Sanderson makes use of the distinction between formal and material sin in so many words, but it is quite clear from what they have written that they associate inculpability always with invincible ignorance.[2]

We see, therefore, that the distinction between formal and material sin depends upon two facts: (1) that a sin committed in invincible ignorance is not blameworthy, and (2) that a sin committed under duress is not blameworthy. Such are material but not formal sins, in the terms of moral theology. Let us consider these two points. First, a sinful 'act' (using that word to cover words and deliberately harboured thoughts) done in invincible ignorance is not culpable, invincible ignorance being lack of knowledge, which could not reasonably be expected of the agent. For example, John Newton, the author of that well-known hymn, *How sweet the Name of Jesus sounds*, wrote it on the deck of a ship carrying a cargo of slaves, of which he was the owner. Apparently

---

[1] K. E. Kirk: *Some Principles of Moral Theology* (1920), p. 245.
[2] Cf. J. Taylor, *Ductor Dubitantium*, Book I, Chap. 3, Rule 1. R. Sanderson, *On Conscience and Human Law* (ed. C. Wordsworth), p. 234.

it never occurred to him that there was anything inconsistent between the two. In those days it was assumed that there was nothing wrong in owning slaves, provided, of course, that they were not ill-treated. After all, slavery, as such, is nowhere condemned in the New Testament. Consequently, Newton's conduct in this matter must be regarded by the moral theologian as materially but not formally sinful; for in these days the Christian conscience, further enlightened by the Holy Spirit, condemns slavery as sinful in any circumstances, being inconsistent with the Christian doctrine of man. If, therefore, Newton had been living today, he could no longer plead invincible ignorance.

To take another example, the Roman soldiers who nailed our Lord to the Cross were not themselves blame-worthy, any more than the modern hangman is where capital punishment exists. They crucified the King of Glory in invincible ignorance. Their action was materially but not formally sinful. But it was otherwise with the chief priests. It may be said that, although they acted in ignorance, it was vincible ignorance. Hence they needed forgiveness; they needed our Lord's prayer: 'Father, forgive them, for they know not what they do' (S. Luke 23.34). Their sin was formal, and not material.

This distinction is applicable to many evil deeds which have been performed in the past, and to many which are performed today. Many wrong deeds have been done by people 'with good intentions', who, as the phrase is, 'didn't know any better'. Indeed, almost every day of our lives we come across instances of this. In practice, it is usually impossible for us to judge in this matter; nor, fortunately, is it necessary that we should. For the priest, however, especially, but not only, in the confessional, it is essential; and it will sometimes be his unpleasant duty to enlighten his penitents, and thus transfer some of their actions from the category of material sin to the category of formal sin. A case of this kind arises frequently today in the Roman Catholic Church where the use of contraceptives is still forbidden by authority but (it would seem) frequently practised by those who do not submit the sin in confession. The confessor here has to face an awkward question about which something has been said in a previous chapter.[1]

In such cases, the confessor has to weigh the circumstances with great care. If the error leads to serious ill consequences, the ignorance must be removed, if thereby the ill consequences can also be removed. Otherwise, as Jeremy Taylor says, 'the error must be opened or not opened, according to prudent considerations relating to the person and his state of affairs. So that the error must rather be suffered than a grievous scandal, or an intolerable or a very great inconvenience'.[2] Here we have, once more, the choice between two evils.

Turning to the second factor, any action performed under duress of any kind, although it is *per se* wrong, is not blameworthy. For instance, take the case already quoted, where a girl under hypnosis was told to strip in front of a class of students on waking up. If she had done this (which in fact she did not) she would probably have been guilty only of material sin, since the immodest act would not have been freely performed. It would have been in a different category from that of a girl who was a 'strip tease' artist. Similarly a person who signs a dishonest contract at the point of a pistol could hardly be said to be guilty of formal sin; although it is sometimes very difficult to say at what point the precise degree of duress which will exculpate the agent is reached. In the last world war, those who worked in concentration camps excused themselves for committing acts of brutality on the ground that they were forced to do them by their superiors. Many will think that in such circum-

---

[1] See p. 75 *supra*.   [2] *Ductor Dubitantium*, Book I, Chap. 3, Rule 8.

stances they should have refused even at the risk of their
lives. Others may judge that this is too much to ask; but
nearly everybody will agree, I think, that no amount of
duress could excuse the performance of diabolical acts of
torture. Ultimately, it is not a primary task of the moral
theologian to settle this problem in any given case. He is
chiefly concerned to make clear the valid distinction
between formal and material sin, for this is a distinction
which follows logically from the doctrine of invincible
ignorance and is valid altogether apart from the question
of duress.

Finally, something must be said concerning what the
moral theologian calls occasions of sin. All sins are
committed in a certain set of circumstances; these
circumstances are known technically as 'occasions of
sin'. An occasion of sin may and often does involve the
presence of specific persons or a specific person. Occasions of sin are classified in four main groups: Remote and
Proximate, Free and Necessary. A remote occasion of
sin is a set of circumstances in which a given individual is
unlikely to be tempted strongly. A proximate occasion of
sin, on the other hand, is one in which a given individual
is extremely likely to fall into sin. Thus it is clear that
occasions of sin vary from individual to individual. For
example, the bar of a public house is certainly a remote
occasion of sin to a person who has never drunk too much
in a long life; but it is a proximate occasion to a heavy
drinker.

The distinction between a free occasion and a necessary occasion is that the former is a set of circumstances
which a person can easily avoid if he wishes, whereas the
latter is a set of circumstances which cannot be avoided
without great loss or great difficulty. For example, if a
person is prone to excessive gambling he does not have to
attend race meetings. For him they are free occasions of
sin. But if he works on a race course and earns his living

there, they are a necessary occasion of sin to him. When an occasion of sin is both free and proximate there is no great problem. The individual concerned is bound in conscience to avoid it. But when it is both proximate and necessary the problem is acute. The individual must seek every opportunity to get away from the temptation—for example, by changing his job—as soon as possible. In the meantime he must do the best that he possibly can to avoid succumbing to the temptation; but the situation may be agonising.

We may illustrate these distinctions further by saying something about an urgent moral problem of today, drug taking and drug addiction. These drugs fall into three main groups, in an ascending order of harmfulness. First comes the smoking of 'reefers' *i.e.* cigarettes of hashish or marijuana. Some are inclined to make light of the use of this drug and to claim that it is non-addictive. Secondly is the use of the drug known as dexedrine one of the amphetamine group of drugs. This stimulant is mixed with a sedative in the so-called 'purple-hearts'. These provide a potent 'boost' which is so strong, when taken in large doses, that almost inevitably those who take them proceed to 'kick over the traces' in one direction or another, and all moral standards disappear when they are under their influence. In this group also may be included the dangerous drug known as L.S.D. 25 (Lysergic acid), which is 'revelatory'. In the third place, there are the opium drugs, especially morphine and heroin. These drugs are addictive in the highest degree, and any reduction in the amount taken leads to terrible 'withdrawal symptoms' which force the addict to such a state of mind that at all costs he must be sure of getting 'the next dose'. Life becomes slavery to a syringe and the fear that the next dose may not be forthcoming. The heroin addict lives for one thing and one thing only—the next dose.

So far as the second and third of these two classes of

drug is concerned, it is clear that to take these drugs is a grave sin, involving as they do the undermining of all moral standards and even endangering life itself. But what is the moral theologian to say regarding the first group? The answer is that it is beyond question a proximate occasion of sin, because, although this drug is not in itself addictive, it awakens the appetite for drug taking, which only too often leads on to other more harmful drugs. As a proximate occasion of sin it must be avoided. The Christian must never run into avoidable temptation. The Lord's Prayer is enough to prove that.

In his treatment of sin, however, the moral theologian or pastor will always try to avoid a purely negative and condemnatory attitude. He will remember the words of the philosopher Spinoza when he said that he sought neither to laugh nor to weep but to understand. He will recognise that the best way to deal with sin is to help people to find something better to put in its place. Thus, for example, one reason why the temperate man does not get drunk is that he has got something better to do. The reason why the philanthropist does not spend all his money on himself is that he has found something better to do with it, and so forth. Contrariwise, the reason why so many young people are strongly tempted to take drugs is that they are driven to it by sheer boredom and a desire for excitement—boredom born of a sense of frustration and fear which is the result of living in a sick society which, having lost its ideals, is vainly seeking a satisfying way of life. Too many of these young people find themselves living in a world without hope, over which hangs all the time the terrible threat of nuclear destruction. It is, therefore, the primary task of the Christian priest and pastor, in all his dealings with sinners, to help them to see that sin is not to be rooted out but to be crowded out.

6

Punishment and Forgiveness

IT WILL be convenient to take as the basis of our discussion the Biblical conception of punishment; and of forgiveness, which is associated with it. As we have seen in the previous chapter, the penalty for deliberate breach of the Covenant, according to Old Testament teaching, was expulsion from the Covenant relationship, and that meant complete destruction. This was due to the manifestation of the wrath, or anger of God. So, for example, the author of Deuteronomy wrote: 'Also in Horeb ye provoked the Lord to wrath, and the Lord was angry with you to have destroyed you.'[1] Similarly the Psalmist could say—'As for transgressors, they shall be destroyed together; the latter end of the wicked shall be cut off.'[2] Forgiveness, on the other hand, is the turning away of wrath by 'the covering of sin'. This might seem to mean the total remission of punishment, because forgiveness and punishment appear to be mutually contradictory ideas; but it did not necessarily mean that. It might involve rather the diminution of punishment, which was then conceived as chastening and not destruction. For example, another Psalmist wrote: 'But he, being full of compassion, forgave their iniquity, and destroyed them not: yea many a time turned he his anger away, and did not stir up *all* his wrath.'[3] As Davidson says, God's anger is not an attribute, like his righteous-

---

[1] Deut. 9.8.   [2] Psalm 37.38.   [3] Psalm 78.38.

ness. 'Wrath in God is what it is in men—an affection, a pathos,—and is transient. But as wrath is but an affection, and not the fundamental character of the divine mind, which rather is long-suffering and compassion, this prevailing disposition may so restrain the anger that no chastisement follows.'[1] So the prayer, 'In wrath remember mercy'[2] is fully intelligible.

We may say, therefore, that, while punishment can be disciplinary and remedial, like the discipline which the human father metes out to his child, as the author of the Book of Proverbs says,[3] it is basically the reaction of the good and holy God to evil. . . . 'Thou art of purer eyes than to behold evil, and canst not look on iniquity.'[4] As another Psalmist says: 'God is a righteous judge, yea a God that hath indignation every day.'[5]

This means that punishment is basically retributive. The wicked are punished because they deserve to be punished. 'Thou shalt reward the proud after their deserving.' The Hebrews were not philosophically minded and did not consciously think out the basic nature of punishment and retribution, but this implication of their teaching on this subject can hardly be questioned. The famous *lex talionis* shows that they thought of this retribution as being made according to the principle of equal justice—an eye for an eye, a tooth for a tooth—no more and no less. It was owing to the fact that this basic belief was so deeply rooted in the minds of the Hebrews that the problem of innocent suffering was felt so acutely by many thoughtful writers among them. They felt that somehow or other this doctrine must be made to square with the facts, the outstanding illustration of this being the Book of Job. And we feel the same today because the principle of justice is implanted in the nature of us all.

[1] *Op. cit.*, p. 332. [2] Habakkuk 3.2. [3] Proverbs 3.1112.
[4] Habakkuk 1.13 (AV). [5] Psalm 7.11.

When we come to the New Testament, we find basically the same ideas. In one of the earliest New Testament
writings S. Paul puts the matter succinctly. Writing of
our Lord's second coming to judgement, he speaks of
him as 'rendering vengeance to them that know not God,
and to them that obey not the gospel of our Lord Jesus:
who shall suffer punishment even eternal destruction
from the face of the Lord and from the glory of his
might'.[1] This is our Lord's teaching also: for example,
speaking of those killed by the fall of the tower of Siloam,
he said: 'Except ye repent, ye shall all likewise perish.'[2]
But in the New Testament the complementary truth of
the Divine Compassion, which at times in the Old Testament seemed to be almost forgotten, shines forth in all
its glory in the life and teaching, and death of our Lord
Jesus Christ. This antithesis, according to the New
Testament, does not amount to a contradiction. The love
of God is not incompatible with the wrath of God, as the
significant expression in the Apocalypse, 'the wrath of the
Lamb', clearly shows. And it is a superficial conception of
the love of God which fails to recognise this truth. Love
is not easy-going indifference to sin.[3] Far from it: the
greater the love, the greater the horror of everything
which can defile or disfigure the object of that love. This
our experience clearly shows to be true.

This point is of such great importance that we must
enlarge upon it a little.

Love must be carefully distinguished from easy going
tolerance, which 'lets off' the offender because it does not
really care. The state of mind which can refer to the
Almighty as 'He's a Good Fellow, and 'twill all be well'[4]
is poles apart from the doctrine that God is love. The
former is the doctrine of a God who despises his creatures.
On the contrary because God *is* love, therefore he must

---

[1] 2 Thess. 1.8 and 9; *cf.* 2 Peter 3.9.   [2] S. Luke 13.5
[3] Hebrews 12.5–12.   [4] E. Fitzgerald, *Omar Khayyam*, Ed. 1. LXIV.

punish, and thereby show that he *does* care. No modern writer has more clearly expressed this truth than Archbishop Temple. He wrote: 'There is certainly severity in Christ's doctrine of God. It is the severity of love, but the love is very severe. Indeed, it is all the more terrible because of its total freedom from personal ill-will; that might be placated; but the antagonism of utter love against selfishness can never be placated. If a man is selfish, and to the degree in which a man is selfish, God is his antagonist. The Father does not desire his suffering or his destruction; He desires only to win him out of his selfishness. But for very love, knowing that love is life and selfishness is death, He shows relentless sternness towards those that are unloving. "His lord delivered him to the tormentors . . . so also shall my heavenly Father do unto you if you forgive not each one his brother from your hearts." It is noticeable, however, that, with the exception of the words just quoted, which occur in connexion with a parable, our Lord does not speak of the Father as inflicting punishment by His own action. Judgement, indeed, is expressly stated to be a function of the Son, not of the Father (S. John 5.22) and, even so, it is not the purpose of the Son or His deliberate act (S. John 3.17; 8.15); rather it is the inevitable consequence of His coming among men with the offer of true life(S. John 3.19). To reject that offer is to be condemned.'[1] Temple goes on to show that the Christian doctrine of 'non-resistance' does not conflict with this. Non-resistance, he says, 'is no mere amiability which accepts an injury rather than face unpleasantness. It is the method of active love'[2]—a serious attempt to make my adversary see in himself the evil that I see in him. It is, in fact, punishment in its most effective form, the vindication of truth and justice from which there is no evasion and no escape. Temple concludes: 'The Gospel of God's undiscriminat-

[1] W. Temple: *Christus Veritas* (1924), p. 182.　　　[2] *Ibid.*, p. 183.

ing love has no syllable of consolation for the self-complacent, except in so far as it assures them that the aim of whatever judgement may befall them is to afford a new opportunity for living as they have no desire to live.'[1]

Generally speaking, the foregoing ideas do not accord with the temper and fashion of modern thinking and argument on this subject, which commonly seems to take it for granted that punishment is either simply deterrent or reformative. That is undoubtedly one of the reasons, perhaps the main reason, why capital punishment is out of favour at the present time: for obviously there can be no question of reforming a murderer, at any rate in this life by executing him, although, indeed, the threat of the death penalty might have an ameliorative influence on the would-be murderer. That is why the question of capital punishment is nowadays usually argued as to whether or not the death penalty is the most effective deterrent.

In spite of what has been said, however, there is definite evidence that deep down in the minds of many people, at least, is the thought of retribution. This came out clearly when the Report of the Commission of Enquiry into the Aberfan disaster was first published. In a television programme which appeared on the evening of the day when the Report was published some of those who took part in the programme and who had lost members of their family in the disaster made it plain that there was a strong feeling that those who were guilty of culpable negligence and who were 'named' in the Report deserved to be punished.

When we enquire why the idea of punishment as retributive is generally out of favour today, however, we find that this is because it is commonly associated with the conception of personal vengeance and vindictiveness, which are widely held to be unworthy and outmoded

[1] W. Temple: *Christus Veritas* (1924), p. 185.

ideas. There is a serious confusion of thought here. No doubt, among primitive peoples retribution was equated with personal vindictiveness, but that the latter is not the root of the idea of retribution is clear from the fact that, as civilisation has advanced, punishment has been taken out of the hands of the injured party or parties and transferred to the courts of justice, which exist to uphold impartial justice and not personal retaliation. Consequently punishment must be administered even against the will of the injured party. For example, if a man's wife is murdered, he is not free to direct the civil power by saying: 'Never mind. I wish to overlook this; please take no action.' Punishment must be meted out to the murderer when he is convicted of the crime, irrespective of the wishes of the next of kin; for punishment is the vindication of just law and not a matter of personal retaliation. That the motives of reform and deterrence may also operate is not to be denied. But the essential question is whether these in themselves afford an adequate basis for punishment, and the answer would seem to be that they do not. Thus punishment will reform the offender only if he recognises that he *deserves* to be punished. Otherwise it will only serve to embitter him. Like the penitent thief he must recognise that he is receiving 'the just reward for his deeds'. As for the motive of deterrence, as Mackenzie says, 'it could scarcely be regarded as just to inflict pain on one man *merely* for the benefit of others. It would involve treating a man as a *thing*, as a mere means, not an end in himself'.[1]

Mackenzie sums the matter up justly when he says: 'Suppose a society had a law against stealing and yet allowed a thief who was unable to make restitution to escape scot-free. The laws of such a society would be little more than injunctions or recommendations to citizens. They would not have the force of imperatives,

---

[1] J. S. Mackenzie: *Manual of Ethics* (6th edn., 1950), p. 374.

or at least they would be imperatives which are liable to exceptions. Absolute imperatives must either be able to prevent every violation of their commands, or else must in some way vindicate their authority when they are violated. This seems to be the primary aim of punishment.'[1] He then goes on to point out what we have already said, that this aim really underlies the other two, since 'neither reformation nor prevention is likely to be effected by punishment unless it is recognised that the punishment is a vindication of the law'[2] *i.e.* of justice.

Bishop Butler has clearly shown that the emotion of resentment against injury and injustice is both natural in man and good, and is one of the common bonds by which society is held together. It is only the 'excess and abuse of this natural feeling, in cases of personal and private injury'[3] which is wrong. He goes on to point out that 'it is of the very nature of this vice to propagate itself, not only by way of example, which it does in common with other vices, but in a peculiar way of its own; for resentment itself, as well as what is done in consequence of it, is the object of resentment; hence it comes to pass, that the first offence, even when so slight as to be dropped and forgotten, becomes the occasion of entering into a long intercourse of ill offices: neither is it at all uncommon to see persons, in this progress of strife and variance, change parts: and him who was at first the injured person, become more injurious and blamable than the aggressor'.[4] Nevertheless, resentment is not inconsistent with good will, for, as Butler points out, we often see both together in the relationship between parents and children and in other human relationships.

Before we pass on to consider the question of forgiveness, something must be said about capital punish-

---

[1] *Op. cit.*, p. 376.   [2] *Ibid.*   [3] Sermon VIII upon *Resentment*.
[4] Sermon IX on *Forgiveness of Injuries*.

ment. So far as I know, this has never been formally condemned by the Church in any synod or council as *per se* wrong, although, of course, there have been and are now many Christians who do not approve of it. When it has been defended, this has been on one or both of two grounds. The first is the passage in Genesis which says: 'Whoso sheddeth man's blood, by man shall his blood be shed.'[1] To say the least, this is not a very strong argument, for it could be quoted in support of the practice of private vengeance quite as much as for the imposition of the death penalty by the state. Moreover, in these days few scholars would care to found an argument by merely quoting a text from the Old Testament. It is, therefore, rather surprising that recourse has not been made more often to a considerably stronger Biblical argument for capital punishment, and that is our Lord's teaching about the *lex talionis*—'an eye for an eye, a tooth for a tooth'.[2] It will be remembered that when he refers to this in the Sermon on the Mount he does not quote it in full, when he sets it aside, but omits the first clause, 'life shall go for life'. It is true that our Lord is not now directly concerned with the question of punishment but with the way in which his followers should bear insults, telling them not to resent them but to ignore them by turning the other cheek. Nevertheless, by omitting in this context all reference to the clause on which the rabbis based their legitimisation of capital punishment, it could be plausibly argued that, by implication, he is thereby endorsing this part of the Jewish law. At that time the literal application of the other parts of the *lex talionis* had been commuted for a money payment; but for homicide the law was still literally interpreted. Consequently a much stronger argument for capital punishment can be put forward on the basis of this passage than on the text from Genesis.

[1] Genesis 9.6.   [2] Deut. 19.21 cf. Exod. 21.23 and 24.

K

The second ground on which the lawfulness of capital punishment is based is that put forward by Aquinas. He says: 'So we see that, if for the health of the whole body it is advisable to cut off one of its members, say because it is rotten or corrupted, it can be lawfully and for the sake of health cut off. But any individual person is related to the whole community as a part to the whole. Therefore if any person is a danger to the community and a corruptor of it owing to some sin he can be lawfully and for the sake of the community killed, that the common good may be preserved; for as it is said in 1 Corinthians 5.6 "A little leaven corrupts the whole lump." '[1] This argument is better than that built on the passage in Genesis, but it is not entirely satisfactory, because it is by no means clear that a murderer is a greater danger to society than some other kinds of evil men—*e.g.* the pimp, the procurer, or even the promoter of vast gambling concerns and the cigarette manufacturer. Yet few people probably would hold that these should be liable to capital punishment, as the argument of Aquinas might seem to suggest. Moreover, in any case this argument does not *demand* capital punishment but merely permits it.

It would seem, therefore, that ultimately we are forced to deal with this question on grounds of expediency, if we think that capital punishment is not *per se* ruled out as immoral, as of course many people think it is. They hold that the sanctity of human life is such that it is the prerogative of God alone to take it and consequently that capital punishment is always wrong even as suicide is always wrong.

Furthermore, the practice of capital punishment (they hold) does not a little to weaken in the public mind this reverence for human life, and is wrong for that reason also.

[1] *Summa Theologica*, IIa IIae Q. LXIV, a.2.

Assuming, however, that these arguments do not carry conviction, we have to consider whether or not capital punishment is demanded as a deterrent: not, of course, solely on that ground—since it would be immoral to use a person simply as a means—but as a deterrent based on the belief in the doctrine of just retribution. In this matter it is not easy to obtain clear evidence; but on the whole it seems that in those countries in which the death penalty has been abolished there has been no notable increase in capital crime. A case can, therefore, certainly be made for the position that capital punishment should not be retained on the ground that it is the most effective deterrent against homicide.[1] One thing seems to be pretty clear—especially so far as the Church of England is concerned—and that is that opinion has gradually been hardening against the legitimacy of imposing the death penalty. Indeed, to us today it is almost incredible that when a bill was introduced into Parliament in 1810 to abolish the death penalty for stealing five shillings or more it was defeated, the Archbishop of Canterbury and six other bishops voting against it. On the other hand, when in 1956, the House of Lords debated the question of the suspension or the abolition of the death penalty for murder, both the archbishops and eight out of the nine bishops present voted in favour of it. Six years later this matter was debated in the Upper House of the Convocation of Canterbury when the following motion was unanimously passed:

'That this House would welcome the introduction, and adoption by Parliament, of a bill providing for:

1. The abolition of capital punishment, or at least its complete suspension for a period of five years;

[1] 'The fact that the evidence on this unique deterrent force is far from conclusive would seem to tilt the scales in favour of abolition' P. J. Fitzgerald: *Criminal Law and Punishment* (1962), p. 227.

2. Such punishment and treatment for the convicted person as would assist in his own reclamation and ensure the safety of society;

3. Suitable compensation for the relatives or dependants of the victims of homicide.'[1]

A similar motion was approved in the Lower House of Canterbury, in 1961, and it is probably fair to say that this represents the opinion of the majority of Anglicans today.

We now pass on to consider the nature of forgiveness. The first question which arises is whether it is entirely inconsistent with punishment. The answer must be that it is not, although at first sight it may seem to be. Indeed one of the commonest mistakes in popular ethical thinking is to suppose that forgiveness necessarily involves the remission of the penalty. That is not Biblical ethics. In Holy Scripture forgiveness is *never* identified with the remission of the penalty. They must not be regarded as alternatives. In point of fact there is always a penalty for sin which has to be paid. It is what the well-known hymn calls 'the price of sin'. That penalty must be paid, and always is paid, by somebody, even if, as we shall see later, it is paid vicariously by somebody other than the offender. Even when the offender is completely forgiven by God, the price is paid, and he can never be as if he has not sinned. His character may indeed, in the end, be enriched by the redeeming love of God's pardon: *O felix culpa quae talem et tantum meruit habere redemptorem,*[2] he may be able to exclaim. But he can never be as if he had not sinned. Emphatically forgiveness does not mean the remission of the penalty.

How, then are we to understand forgiveness? The majority of modern theologians equate it with the restoration to fellowship, and, therefore, hold it to be the same as reconciliation. 'To forgive' says William

---

[1] Chronicle of the Convocation of Canterbury, 1962, p. xv.
[2] Latin office for Easter Eve.

Temple,'is to restore to the old relationship. It is because men have pictured God's judgement of souls so much in the likeness of the courts of earthly justice that this has been so often obscured. The prisoner in the dock has never been in any close relationship with the judge on the bench.'[1] Vincent Taylor has argued that this is not the meaning of forgiveness in New Testament usage, maintaining that there it always refers to the removal of the barrier of sin.[2] The distinction is not of importance from our present point of view, because once the barrier is removed the reconciliation takes place; and, in any case, when forgiveness takes place between two human beings it must mean reconciliation rather than the removal of sin, because in this case the wrong is not all on one side as it is in the broken relationship between God and man.

How, then, is this broken relationship healed? The answer is that this is brought about by forgivingness on the part of the injured party and repentance on the part of the offender. Repentance means saying 'I am sorry' and meaning it, and this involves willingness to make amends and to forgive others. As Temple said, we really need two words 'forgivingness' and 'forgivenness'. If we are really sorry, we shall be ready to forgive others and be animated by 'forgivingness' ourselves. Nothing is more strongly emphasised about forgiveness in the New Testament than this. Every time we say the Lord's Prayer we are reminded of it. ('Forgive us our trespasses *as we forgive* . . .')

Before man can be forgiven by God, therefore, he must repent. How is he to be brought to repentance? Temple has clearly explained this in what is perhaps the most profound discussion of the nature of forgiveness since R. C. Moberly's famous *Atonement and Personality.*

[1] W. Temple: *Christus Veritas* (1924), p. 257.
[2] V. Taylor: *Forgiveness and Reconciliation* (1941), p. 4.

Temple wrote: 'After all, others have taught that for-giveness follows repentance: what no other could do was to secure that repentance should follow sin. But Christ has done this for all who believe that in Him we see the Father. Fear of punishment might deter me from sinful action, but it could not change my sinful desires: on the contrary, it would be more likely to intensify them by the action of that psychological law described by St. Paul which we have lately learned to call the Law of Reversed Effort. But to realise what my selfishness means to the Father who loves me with a love such as Christ reveals, fills me with horror of the selfishness and calls out an answering love.'[1]

However, although repentance is essential for forgive-ness, we know that our repentance is never complete and full. There is no question of winning or deserving our forgiveness from God. This is a point which is apt to be overlooked, as, for example, it is by Rashdall when he argues that the only requirement for forgiveness is repentance, without any necessary reference to the atoning work of Christ.[2] As Moberly argues so forcibly, our Lord is the only true penitent; for penitence means dissociating ourselves entirely from the sin and this is something which no sinner can do completely. In order to repudiate sin fully a person must be entirely free from it and this is true of our Lord alone, as Christians believe. That is why Christians have always believed that they receive their forgiveness only through the merits of their Redeemer.

This is New Testament teaching. We are forgiven for Christ's sake.[3] It was part of the earliest Christian tradi-tion which was delivered to S. Paul when he became a Christian that 'Christ died for our sins according to the Scriptures',[4] and that we share the benefits of Christ's

---

[1] *Op. cit.*, p. 263.   [2] H. Rashdall: *The Idea of the Atonement* (1929), pp. 24ff.
[3] Ephes. 1.7, 4.32; Col. 1.14; 1 John 2.12.   [4] 1 Cor. 15.3.

death through being buried with him in holy baptism. As the Nicene Creed says, there is 'one baptism for the remission of sins'.

This teaching involves a set of ideas which lie at the very heart of the doctrine of forgiveness and they are those associated with the conception of vicarious suffering and sacrifice. As we have seen, punishment always follows upon sin, and in our hearts we know that this is right. But sometimes the punishment is borne not only vicariously but also willingly. When that happens, it may have a redemptive value which wins the sinner to sorrow for his sin. Our human experience clearly shows this to be the case. When the prodigal son returned home and was freely forgiven by his father, as he looked into his father's face he knew at once that 'he had borne his griefs and carried his sorrows'; and it was that knowledge which made his repentance as complete as it could be for such a man as he. Such was the sacrifice of our Lord, which, Christians believe, was a vicarious bearing of the sin of the world. So he was called the Lamb of God. Christians look at Christ on the Cross as the returned prodigal looked in the face of his father.

What, then, of sin committed after baptism? At first, this was regarded as unthinkable, at least by some Christians. One of them was the author of the First Epistle of John. He wrote: 'Whosoever is begotten of God doeth no sin, because his seed abideth in him: and he cannot sin because he is begotten of God.'[1] But the facts could not be reconciled with this position, and the author of the Epistle to the Hebrews could write: 'For as touching those who were once enlightened and tasted of the heavenly gift, and were made partakers of the Holy Ghost, and tasted the good word of God, and the powers of the age to come, and then fell away, it is impossible to renew them again unto repentance.'[2] This problem

---

[1] 1 John 3.9., cf. 5.18. [2] Hebrews 6.4.

much exercised the mind of the early Church. The earliest solution seems to have been that which we find in Hermas, that only one repentance was allowed for sin after baptism, and even then not for the sins of apostasy, murder and adultery. Tertullian called this 'the second plank',[1] and, even so, heavy penances were publicly exacted. Reference is made to this practice in the Book of Common Prayer in the Commination Service where we read: 'Brethren, in the primitive Church there was a godly discipline, that, at the beginning of Lent, such persons as stood convicted of notorious sin were put to open penance, and punished in this world, that their souls might be saved in the day of the Lord; and that others, admonished by their example, might be the more afraid to offend.' It goes on to say that it is to be wished that 'the said discipline may be restored again'. Associated with this public penance was confession and absolution, though it has been much debated whether the confession was ever public.

However that may be, the rule of the one penance disappeared during the fifth and the sixth centuries. Bishop Kirk gave it as his opinion that this was due to 'a growing ascendancy of the priesthood in the ministry of absolution'[2] which at first seems to have been the prerogative of the bishops only.

In the very early period little stress seems to have been laid upon the absolution, the emphasis being on the efficacy of repentance or, as it came to be called, 'perfect contrition' in winning forgiveness. As we saw in the last chapter, the instances of Lazarus who was raised up *before* the disciples 'loosed him' and of the lepers who were healed *before* they 'showed themselves to the priest' were understood to mean that repentance by itself was enough to secure forgiveness, provided that it was complete. Importance was, indeed, attached to the

---

[1] *On Repentance*, C.9.   [2] K. E. Kirk: *The Vision of God* (1932), p. 281.

presence of the bishop or the priest, but different views were held as to his precise function, and the form of absolution was precatory and not declaratory until the twelfth century. However, as Kirk rightly says: 'The primitive conception, in short, was too naive to fit the facts. That "perfect contrition" would win immediate forgiveness from God was never denied. But a truer psychology saw how rare such "perfect contrition" must be. Reflection suggested that here was the real ground for the action of the priest in reconciliation—the power of the keys, for so long only dimly understood, would unlock the stores of divine grace as the faulty human heart could not. . . . The priest, who was hitherto spoken of, as often as not, as primarily the witness and helper of the sinner's penitence, now becomes definitely the agent of forgiveness; and the declaratory form of absolution is finally adopted.'[1] For 'agent' here we should surely read 'instrument'. Before long this led to the Paschal Precept, rendering sacramental confession compulsory at Easter, laid down by the Fourth Lateran Council in 1215.

Where does the Anglican stand in this matter? In the first place, we note that the Church of England went back behind the Paschal Precept, about which the Book of Common Prayer is silent. But the instruction in the Office for the Visitation of the Sick in which the sick man is to be 'moved' to make a special confession of his sins, 'if he feel his conscience troubled with any weighty matter' and to receive absolution 'if he humbly and heartily desire it' makes it clear that the confession is voluntary and not obligatory. But secondly, it is to be carefully noted that the declaratory form of absolution is retained.

What, then, is the significance of sacramental confession and absolution as it is presented in the Prayer Book? We have seen that the doctrine that perfect contrition *per se* is the only essential requirement for God's forgiveness

[1] *Op. cit.*, p. 289.

has always persisted in the Church. Even the Council of
Trent explicitly stated this,[1] although sacramental confession was required, when it was obtainable, as being a
law of the Church. The penitent must, therefore,
according to Roman Catholic teaching, fulfil this
requirement at least *in voto* if he is to receive forgiveness,
in spite of the sufficiency of 'perfect contrition'. We, in
the Anglican Church, are not, of course, involved in this
rather self-contradictory position. We are in the happier
position of being able to say concerning sacramental
confession: All may, none must, some should resort to it.
Those who should are those troubled with 'any weighty
matter' of conscience: and no pastor of experience can fail
to have come across many such, or to know how great is
the relief obtained by such persons through confession.
They feel as Christian did in *The Pilgrim's Progress* when
his burden fell from his back before the Cross.

What, then, we must ask, is the theology of absolution
which underlies this practice? Let us take as our starting
point Hooker's statement of the widely held theory that
the absolution is purely declaratory. Hooker wrote: 'As
for the ministerial sentence of private absolution, it can
be no more than a declaration what God hath done; it
hath but the force of the prophet Nathan's absolution,
"God hath taken away thy sin"; than which construction, especially of words judicial, there is not anything
more vulgar. For example, the publicans are said in the
Gospel to have justified God (S. Luke 7.29), the Jews in
Malachi (Mal. 3.15) to have blessed proud men, which
sin and prosper: not that the one did make God righteous, or the other the wicked happy, but to "bless", to
"justify", and to "absolve" are as commonly used for
words of judgement, or declaration, as of true and
real efficacy.'[2] He then proceeds to quote the Master of

---

[1] *Sessio* XIV, C.4.
[2] Hooker: *Laws of Ecclesiastical Polity*, Book VI, Chap. 6.8.

the Sentences, Jerome and other writers in favour of this position.

Hooker, however, in arguing thus, is guilty of two errors. First, he argues, if 'perfect contrition' leads to forgiveness, how can absolution minister the latter to the penitent? Here he makes the common but fatal mistake of confusing true contrition with perfect contrition. Of course it is true, as he says, that the penitent must be truly contrite before he can be forgiven, but this is a very different matter from saying that he must be perfectly contrite. If the penitent is not truly contrite, as far as he, being what he is, can be, he is not rightly disposed to receive absolution; but this, unfortunately, is not at all the same thing as being perfectly contrite. For this to happen he has to turn *completely* from his sin, and this, as he knows only too well, he cannot do. As S. Paul says, when he would do well, evil is present with him. The Anglican, indeed, as we have seen, is not committed to the view that Absolution is essential, as the Roman Catholic Church maintains; but it does not at all follow from this that Absolution is not an efficacious sign of grace, to use the words of the definition of sacraments in Article 28. Hooker's theology of the sacraments, indeed, falls short here, when he makes the unsatisfactory distinction between grace being given 'with' the sacraments but not 'by' the sacraments. Here he entirely ignores the doctrine of the *obex*, which is basic to the doctrine that the sacraments confer the grace of God *ex opere operato*. It runs as follows: *Ex ipsa valida administratione sacramenti, dummodo ne adsit obex*. And the *obex* is defined as the lack of either of the essential dispositions for receiving the sacraments rightly—*i.e.* faith and repentance. The sacraments are not magic, although they have often been misrepresented as being such.

It is because Hooker ignores the doctrine of the *obex* that he falls into his second error, when he asks: 'What needeth observation whether penitents have worthiness and bring contrition, if the words of absolution do infuse contrition ?'[1]

The answer is, as we have seen, a very simple one. According to the doctrine that absolution confers grace, this only happens when the penitent is rightly disposed, *i.e.* when he is sincerely (which does not mean completely) penitent.

In my view the doctrine that absolution is *only* declaratory means that sacramental confession fails in what, according to the Prayer Book, is its essential purpose, which is to bring peace and assurance to the person with a troubled conscience. Often it is not enough to tell such a person that if he truly repents him of his sin he is, so to say, automatically forgiven by God. His difficulty frequently is precisely that he cannot be sure that he *does* really repent of his sin, and that he is truly contrite. What he needs then is some means of assuring him that the deficiency of his penitence is made good by the grace of God; and this is exactly what the 'benefit of absolution' does. It would seem, therefore, that the declaratory doctrine of absolution breaks down at the critical point, and is not consistent with the teaching of the Prayer Book. Perhaps not due weight has been given by advocates of this theory to the fact that at the Reformation the Church of England retained the formula 'I absolve thee', which obviously is much more impressive than is the precatory form which might, in theory at least, be used by anybody and not be reserved to the bishop or the priest.

[1] *Op. cit.*, Book VI, Chap. 6.13.

7

The Christian Standard and Ideal

THE CHRISTIAN moral ideal is Our Lord Jesus Christ. Of that there can be no question at all. Christ is the one perfect example. As Bishop Hensley Henson once said, Christ alone of all the great moral teachers and founders of religions is able to offer himself as a model and example of his own teaching. Accordingly we find in the Holy Scripture, as well as elsewhere, deeply embedded the *Imitatio Christi* motive. As S. Peter says, 'Christ left us an example that you should follow his steps.'[1] Yet it is manifest that this cannot mean a literal example for all men to follow. For instance, Our Lord was a celibate and lived the life of a wandering evangelist. Clearly this life is not intended by God to be the kind of life to be lived by everybody. If it were, in a short time there would be nobody left to live it. And once this admission is made, it becomes necessary to show how, so to say, this Christ-life can be transposed to another key and so adapted to other circumstances. This raises many difficulties.

The Christian Church very soon began to set about this task, and this led to the formulation of the Christian ideal in terms of the several virtues. First and foremost were the so-called three theological virtues of faith, hope

[1] 1 Peter 2.21.

and charity, which trio makes its first appearance in the earliest book of the New Testament (1 Thess. 1.3) and this is remarkably early. Soon there were added to these the four pre-Christian cardinal virtues of justice, prudence, courage and temperance (Wisdom 8.7) in a Christian dress, thus producing the sevenfold gift of God the Holy Spirit, another pre-Christian idea (Isaiah 11) baptised into Christ.

In all the traditional standard works on moral theology we find this analysis of the Christian ideal followed and expounded.

At the present day, however, the demand is increasingly being made that the Christian ethic and the Christian standard should be expressed in terms of love alone. This is specially noticeable in certain modern Anglican writers. It is not perhaps always remembered that there is nothing new in the belief in the primacy of love. But everything turns on what is meant by love. One of the earliest works on the subject of the Christian moral standard has love as its main theme; it was written by S. Augustine, *De Moribus Ecclesiae Catholicae*, a profound and illuminating work, written in opposition to the dualism of the Manichees. The teaching of the latter is not, in these days, what William James once called 'a live option' so that we need not here concern ourselves with that aspect of Augustine's treatise. But it will suit our purpose very well to make what he has said in this book about love the starting-point of our treatment of the Christian moral standard.

S. Augustine sets out from the fact that we all seek happiness. Every person normally does that. But, Augustine argues, you cannot be happy unless you have what you love, whatever that may be. Nor is anybody really happy if, although he has what he loves, the latter is bad (*noxium*). Nor, again, is anybody happy if he does not desire what he ought to desire. In that case his condition is morbid. In none of these three instances is a person really happy. There is, however, a fourth possibility, and this is realised when what is man's good is both loved and possessed. This is true enjoyment and happiness.

So we have to ask what is man's best good. Nobody can doubt, Augustine argues, that what we call virtue leads to this. But nothing (he says), is virtue if it is not the supreme love of God. 'God is for us the "*Summum bonum*" ' (*op. cit.*, I C.8). He argues that the four great virtues—commonly known as the cardinal virtues— make this clear. Temperance is keeping love inviolate; courage is love bearing all things for the sake of the Beloved; justice is service of the loved one alone and on that account ruling rightly; prudence is wisely choosing between those things which may help and those which may hinder love (*ibid.*, C.15).

Consequently, since to seek the highest good is to love well, clearly this is nothing else than to seek God with the whole heart, the whole soul and the whole mind, and to keep this love incorruptible by 'the several virtues'. 'What more can I say about morality?' he concludes, 'For if God is the *summum bonum* of man (which cannot be denied) it follows forthwith, since to seek the *summum bonum* is to live well, that this latter is nothing else but to love with the whole heart, the whole soul, and the whole mind God from whom it comes to pass that love is preserved in him whole and undefiled'(C.25).

Augustine then turns to consider what is meant by loving ourselves in the second great command to love our neighbour as ourselves. He says that nobody who loves God can fail to love himself; indeed, only he who loves God knows how to love himself. For to love oneself properly means to behave so as to enjoy the good, which is God. Thus there is no surer step towards loving God than to love others as yourself. But you only love yourself properly if you love God more than yourself. What, therefore you do for yourself must also be done in relation to your neighbour, that is, so that he also may love God properly. For you do not love him as yourself unless you try to lead him to that good which you yourself seek. That is why S. Paul says that love works no ill to our neighbour (*ibid.* C.26).

Thus far S. Augustine. In his whole treatment of this subject we see how God-centred is his theology—entirely different, indeed, from much of the modern discussion of the place of love in Christian morality. In these days, again and again this is argued merely on the human level. We are told to treat others as persons; we are to treat them as individuals. This it is to love them. Indeed (so we are told), we must deal with every moral problem as it concerns this particular individual in these specific circumstances. This, it is argued, is the meaning of Christian love. It cannot really be expressed in laws and rules. Each case must be dealt with on its merits. Love will never pass judgement on the basis of general laws. It may sometimes be right for *this* person to commit adultery; for *this* person to anticipate marriage; for *this* married person to seek sexual intercourse outside marriage; even for *this* person to commit an abortion. Love, we are told, must be experimental and 'spontaneous'. 'Without spontaneity in action we are not responsible moral agents in the liberty with which Christ has set us free.'[1] This way of thinking has been not uncommon among certain modern Anglican moralists, who are very anxious to avail themselves of the Augustinian dictum, *Dilige et quod vis fac*. But such writers, in arguing that if spontaneous love is the motive, that is what is of primary importance, conveniently forget that Augustine meant by *dilectio* something which is basically divine and God-centred; in fact, something very different from what they mean.

---

[1] F. R. Barry, *Christian Ethics and Secular Society* (1966), p. 102.

Indeed, I suspect that many of them have never read what S. Augustine wrote about this.

It is true that S. John wrote: 'He who loveth not his brother whom he has seen cannot love God whom he has not seen'; but we must not infer from this that our human relations afford us the true criterion of love. That was not S. John's meaning at all; for he tells us that love is *per se* divine. 'God is love', and 'Love is of God' he tells us. To make love of our neighbour theologically primary is, therefore, to turn things upside down. S. John's often quoted remark is not intended to do that, but merely to draw attention to the fact that, *in order of time*, human beings generally come to learn of the love of God through the love of man; but *in order of thought*, the love of God is and must always be primary.

God, indeed, S. John says, is love. By this he makes it objective, not subjective; divine, not human. S. Augustine reiterates this, and by so doing shows that the fact that love is for the Christian the supreme guide of human conduct does not at all lead to the conclusion, which too many modern moralists are inclined to draw, that all moral laws and rules are thereby rendered obsolete or at least of secondary importance. They have been led to this false conclusion simply because they have made *human* love their criterion, and this is, as we have seen, basically false.

The great moral laws and principles remain; for they are the expression of the Divine Being. Law and love must never be put in mutual opposition. If we say that God is love, as S. John does, we are, indeed, using a term which is strictly indefinable. Love is what God, the *Ens Realissimum* is, but we cannot define it or God; for to define is to limit, and God is infinite. Yet nothing that the New Testament says about 'love' carries with it the subjective or individualistic moralism of some modern professedly Christian moralists. This doctrine of the objectivity and transcendence of love is one of crucial importance, and we must elaborate it further in order to bring out its fuller meaning.

We have just said that love is, in strictness, indefinable, because it is ultimate. Nevertheless, it is a phenomenon which is familiar to everybody, and we can draw out its meaning by considering the evidence of our common experience.

The first feature to be noticed is that love *per se* points to the infinite. This has been clearly perceived by the greatest minds. Dante, for example, ends his great *Divine Comedy* by speaking of 'Love that moves the sun and the other stars.'[1] God is the true object of all love.[2] This is shown by two facts of experience. The first is that love of our human friends will become selfish and degenerate unless it is combined with the love of God.

> I could not love thee (Dear) so much
> Loved I not honour more.[3]

Many and many a person who has idolised a human relative or friend has in bitterness at the last discovered this.

The other fact is that we never, so to say, come to the end of loving. We can never say 'I have loved so and so enough: it is time to stop.' 'Love never faileth.'[4] 'Many waters cannot quench love.'[5]

The second characteristic of love to be noticed is that all love is one; whether it is the love of parent and child, of husband and wife, or between friends, or between man and God.[6] This truth is often obscured because our human loves are tainted by selfishness; yet it is not the love which is at fault but the selfishness. Love, in so far as it is true to itself, seeks only the good of the other. That

[1] *Paradiso*, Canto XXXIII.   [2] *Ibid.*, Canto XXVI.
[3] Richard Lovelace, *To Lucasta, Going to the Wars*.
[4] 1 Corinthians 13.8.   [5] Canticles, 8.7.
[6] Nygren: *Agape and Eros*, goes badly astray here.

is why it is shown in self-sacrifice. Nevertheless, it is a mutual relationship, and it seeks to be reciprocated. Love which is not requited is not perfect love.

This point was the theme of a famous controversy between Fénelon and Bossuet in the seventeenth century when the former argued in favour of the disinterested love of God. But he was sometimes in danger of forgetting that, pressed too far, this doctrine is less than Christian and conforms rather to pantheistic systems of thought, in which 'God' is regarded as an impersonal being, who cannot and does not return our human love.

This brings us to a third characteristic of love. It is the essential mark of personality. 'It is the fundamental characteristic of our personality, the first to appear in infancy, the last to survive in age; our strongest motive, our deepest need, the one desire whose satisfaction is the only condition of our ultimate rest. Personality has, in fact, been described as the capacity for fellowship, which is love . . . consequently all the arguments for the personality of God, which arise from the existence of human personality, are arguments also for the love of God.'[1]

All this human experience of the nature of love is corroborated and exemplified in the incarnate life of the Son of God. There you see a perfectly human life which, in the judgement of many generations of Christians, points beyond itself to God. In that life we see human love at its highest, without discrimination. At the same time we see on the cross that it is more than human: 'Love so amazing, so divine.'

Here, again, we see that love knows no limit. 'He loved them unto the end.' Yet it was, in spite of all, a love that sought to be requited. 'Will you also go away?' pathetically he asks his disciples as the shadows gather round him and his disciples begin to desert him. And we see his longing for companionship when he takes with

[1] J. R. Illingworth: *Christian Character*, p. 88 (1904 edn.).

him to Gethsemane the three chosen friends, although he knows full well that he must go through with this thing alone.

It is not relevant to our purpose here to meet the objections which can be, and have been, urged against the Christian belief that Jesus of Nazareth is the Son of God, and the fullest possible revelation of the nature of God. This is a book of moral theology, and the moral theologian legitimately presupposes the truth of Christian theology. Our purpose now is rather to expound the true nature of that much misunderstood quality which we call 'love', and to show how it affords a standard and an ideal of right conduct. I have tried to show that it can be rightly understood only if we hold fast to the traditional order of the two great commands: Love God and love your neighbour as yourself.

How, then, in practice, does this love work out? Here we come face to face with the oft repeated assertion that this means the end of all moral rules and precepts. This contention is so widespread today that it is superfluous to quote instances. I hope to show, however, that it does not at all follow from the Christian doctrine of the moral primacy of love.

Let us, then, enquire a little more closely into the question of the place of rules in Christian morality and the reasons for the reaction against them. At the outset it is worth while to call to mind an incident in the life of S. Augustine, who is so often quoted to support the modern reaction. It is told by him in his *Confessions*[1] how greatly his mother was upset by his adherence to Manichaean opinions, and how she had a dream in which she was weeping and lamenting, 'with her feet planted on a wooden rule', when she saw coming towards her a radiant youth, who smiled upon her cheerfully. He asked her the reason for her sorrow, and when she said she was

[1] Book 3, Chap. 11.

bewailing her son's perdition, he told her to be of good comfort and look and see. 'She looked, and saw me standing by her side on the same rule', *i.e.* the Rule of Faith, which played such an important part in the life of the early Church. This shows, clearly enough, that in the mind of both Augustine and his mother there was no hostility to the idea of rule in the life of the Christian. Indeed, it is not at first sight at all clear why there should be. A rule is something which is straight, and straightness and goodness are always associated, as are crookedness and evil. Why should it be thought that love is independent of straightness, still less incompatible with it?

It will perhaps be said that love, of course, is not crooked in the moral sense of the term, but that it is not rigid and unbending. Rules and laws, it will be said, are rigid and unbending, in so far as they are rules, and that is why they are wrong. But is this really so? There is a well-known saying that the exception proves the rule. Most rules have exceptions, but this does not prove that rules are wrong or harmful or unnecessary. There is another expression also to be remembered in the present connexion and that is the phrase 'as a rule' which means 'usually' but does not mean 'always'. In fact, life would be quite impossible without rules; and so long as these rules are good and useful rules, they are certainly not incompatible with love. Indeed, human nature being what it is they are the expression of love. A simple example will show this. During the war many of those on active service made a rule to write home at least once a week. This rule ensured that many letters were written which otherwise would never have been written. It was by no means inconsistent with love. Nobody suggested to any man who had made such a rule that this showed that he had no love for his wife. On the contrary, the rule showed that he did care for his wife and was an expression of his love. It is sheer muddled thinking to say that there is any inherent opposition between law and love.

I submit, therefore, that the valid objection to rules is only (*a*) to bad rules and (*b*) to rules which allow of no possible exception. Neither of these objections applies to moral laws and rules as the Christian understands them. There is (for example) a law or rule that we must speak the truth. There are few more important rules for society. If this rule were faithfully kept by all, many social evils would vanish overnight. The fact that there are a few exceptions to this rule (*e.g.* telling a lie to a homicidal maniac with a loaded revolver in order to save somebody's life) in no way alters this. Nor is the position really altered by reason of the fact that the ultimate voice in deciding what these exceptions are to be is the voice of Christian love.

If Christian love be regarded as the pure effulgence of uncreated Light, moral laws and rules are like the colours of the spectrum which make and constitute that pure white beam. There is no antithesis between law and love. The antithesis is between imperfect human laws and love on the one hand, or, between divine moral laws, which reflect the divine Nature, and imperfect human love, on the other. When this question is debated by many modern writers, the laws which are attacked are imperfect man-made laws which it is easy enough to contrast unfavourably with true love, rather than divine, beneficent laws contrasted with counterfeit or, at least, imperfect human love.

As this point is of such crucial importance, it will be well to elucidate it further by taking a specific example— one which is a centre of controversy, viz. the lawfulness of the practice of sexual intercourse outside marriage. Clearly the answer to this question depends ultimately upon what is understood to be the meaning of love. In the New Testament this practice is called *porneia* and it is everywhere condemned in any shape or form. Many moralists today, however, including some claiming to be Christian moralists, are not prepared to do this, asserting that in some circumstances it may be permissible. Before considering their arguments, let us briefly summarise what the New Testament has to say on this matter.

The teaching of the New Testament on the question of extramarital intercourse is quite clear. It carries on the Jewish tradition that *porneia* is sinful. This word is translated 'fornication' in the authorised and revised versions of the English Bible. It is a word derived from the Latin *fornix*, meaning an arch or a vault, because Roman brothels were situated in vaults. Strictly, it means consorting with prostitutes but more generally applies to all extra-marital intercourse. In the R.S.V. it is rendered 'unchastity' or 'immorality'; in the New English Bible, sometimes 'unchastity', sometimes 'sexual immorality' and sometimes 'fornication'. But the meaning is reasonably clear. Extra-marital copulation is forbidden in the New Testament.

This was something which, as we have seen, was nothing new to the Jewish Christians. They took it for granted. But this was far from being the case with Gentile Christians. Some of these had, prior to becoming Christians, been 'God-fearers' *i.e.* proselytes who had shrunk from undergoing the rite of circumcision. These people were drawn to Christianity, especially when they realised that, as Christians, they were under no obligation to be circumcised and were free from the Jewish Law. Many of them, however, went further and made the disastrous mistake of thinking that they were also free to follow the lax sexual habits of the heathen. That was why, when the great Apostolic Decree was made, they were plainly informed that they must abstain from *porneia* (Acts 15.29).

This teaching was not easily assimilated. In the very first of his letters to Gentile Christians S. Paul had to speak plainly about it. 'This is the will of God for you . . . to abstain from fornication.' In other words, every time you say 'Thy will be done' in reciting the Lord's Prayer, you are in fact praying for this. He continues: 'that every single one of you should know how to keep his body pure and reverenced, not in passion and lust, like the heathen who do not know God' (1 Thess. 4. 3–5). In 1 Corinthians S. Paul elaborates this teaching. He says that the body of the Christian is a member of Christ's body (1 Cor. 6.15) and that the bodies of Christians are shrines of the Holy Spirit. This is more than to say that Christians are members of Christ's Body, as he says elsewhere (1 Cor. 12.27). Their *bodies* are members of Christ's body.

It would be impossible to hold a more exalted view of the human body. There is no question of its being unclean or unworthy. All the Greek admiration for the human body is here and more. Unchastity is wrong, not because the body and its desires are evil; but for the opposite reason. Because they are so good they should be instruments, not of self-centred passion, but of self-giving love, which is of God. That is why extra-marital intercourse is excluded. It necessarily springs from something which is less than true love.

Turning now to the teaching of those who are unwilling to condemn the practice of extra-marital intercourse, and who are even willing to commend it in certain circumstances, their position is briefly as follows. There is only one absolute moral criterion, and that is love. When two people commit what is called, or used to be called, fornication (it is argued) it sometimes, perhaps often, happens that they are deeply in love with one another, and hope, when circumstances permit, to marry one another. Why, then, should they be condemned for expressing their love in the most natural way, provided, of course, that they take contraceptive precautions in order not to involve any possible children? They are harming nobody but themselves at the worst. At the best, being passionately drawn together, they achieve real happiness, which in many cases will prove to be lasting. The thrill of sexual intercourse, when carried out with complete mutual satisfaction is indeed in some sense a foretaste of heaven. The Christian moralist who condemns this is held up to contempt as a Puritan and a kill-joy. In the very name of Christian love such intercourse is said to be praiseworthy and not blameworthy. Consequently it is wrong for the Church to condemn extra-marital intercourse out of hand. This is the strongest form of the argument. There is, however, another version which would defend extra-marital intercourse on pragmatic grounds, claiming that sex intercourse is an art (which is true) and that a little practice in it before marriage is likely to facilitate the further acquistion of the art after marriage.[1] This conclusion, however, does not follow, and there is little, if any, evidence to support it. The conclusion does not follow, for the simple reason that intercourse casually or even frivolously carried out either with a prostitute or with a casual acquaintance is an entirely different thing from intercourse with a loved wife. That has been discovered by many a man who has successfully had sexual union before marriage but who, to his dismay, has found himself impotent on the marriage night in the embrace of his chaste wife.

It is of great importance to notice that even the former of these two arguments for extra-marital intercourse is drawn from purely human relationships; from human love, in fact, and not from divine love. This vitiates the argument, because human love, unfortunately, is never

[1] G. M. Carstairs: *This Island Now* (1963), p. 51.

entirely pure and untainted by selfishness. Indeed the very intensity of the pleasure of the fulfilment of sexual desire means that only too easily does it become self-centred. Even in the case of two young lovers inspired by a truly altruistic mutual love, in which there is on both sides a deep sense of being unworthy of the other, when extra-marital intercourse takes place this is due to a selfish desire to enjoy prematurely the physical delight of sex—in a word, to an imperfection and taint in the love. If this taint were not present, the lovers would rather wait until their committal to one another can be complete and final. In other words, the desire to enjoy the body of the other *now*, without any longer delay, is a selfish desire, and not love in the full sense.

If, on the other hand, the argument had begun at the other end—at God's love and not man's—it would appear at once that love means total and complete self-giving, without any possibility or question of drawing back; seeking indeed a response but in no respect dependent on getting that response. At the human level, as we have seen, this self-giving must be complete and accompanied by all the circumstances of finality, with no question of going back; and this is only another way of saying that it must be done in marriage, because that is exactly what monogamous marriage is. It follows from this that the Christian ethic of love, so far from supporting extra-marital sexual intercourse, leads straight to its condemnation. Fornication, in other words, is wrong, because it is not based on true love and mutual self-giving as complete as we can make it.

Let the position which we are maintaining be clearly understood. We are not arguing that love provides the sole justification for sexual intercourse; otherwise it would follow that in societies where 'arranged' marriages are the custom sexual intercourse would not be legitimate, since, *ex hypothesi*, in such marriages love cannot be assumed, to say the least. What we are saying is that the marriage bond alone provides the circumstances in which love can come to full fruition; and that is why sexual intercourse should be confined to marriage. Those who reject this restriction of copulation to marriage may be challenged to say what other restriction is feasible in western civilisation to-day, or whether they are ready to justify what, in my view, is the only real alternative, and that is sexual promiscuity. Are they really prepared to approve the kind of sexual orgy described in Lord Denning's Report on the Profumo affair where the guests at a dinner party take off all their clothes, and, after dining in the nude, proceed to indiscriminate copulation.[1] It is hard to believe that they are; yet that is what sexual promiscuity involves. Surely the line must be drawn somewhere, and, if not at marriage, where can it be drawn?

Returning to our theme, the adoption of the objective standpoint of the divine love casts a reflex light on the experience of human sex love. The physical delights of intercourse between true lovers are hard to exaggerate; they are capable of making even a plain and ordinary woman look beautiful when she is in the arms of her lover. This human ecstasy is a foreshadowing of what will be the bliss of heaven. What the body of a beautiful woman is to her true lover is a dim foreshadowing of what it will be to enjoy the Beatific Vision. Then and not until then shall we know fully the meaning of love.

S. Augustine saw this very clearly. 'But what do I love when I love Thee?' he writes. 'Not bodily form, not temporal splendour, not the beauty of light, all which are a delight to these eyes; not sweet melodies of varied songs, not the sweetness of flowers and ointments and spices; not manna and honey; not human limbs in the longed for carnal embrace. Not these things do I love

[1] *Loc. cit.* p. 108.

when I love my God; and yet I am loving a certain kind
of light, a certain kind of sound, a certain kind of food,
and a certain kind of embrace of my inner man.'[1] Love
of God is none of these things, and yet it includes and
transcends them all. That is why it is always to the Song
of Songs—a collection of love lyrics—that the saints have
turned in order to find words to express their love of God.
However inadequate these words may be, the human
experience which they express is a dim reflexion of the
love of God.

The upshot of all this discussion is that love, as understood by Christians, is not the all too frail, human and
oscillating thing which men exhibit. It represents the
strong, indestructible, and unchangeable nature of God,
the Creator and Maker of all things, and this finds
expression in what we call the laws of morality, which
exclude lying, stealing, fornication and adultery. Nor
does our Lord say anything to suggest otherwise. He does
not speak directly about fornication in the Gospels, but
he does condemn adultery, even to the extent of con-
demning the harbouring of adulterous thoughts (S.
Matthew 5.28.). Rightly understood, the Christian ethic
of love is no soft and sentimental thing: it is the strongest
thing in the universe.

How, then, does our Lord teach us to regard moral
laws and rules? We have seen that in his insistence on the
primacy of love he does not explicitly or implicitly
condemn them *per se*. Yet his moral teaching and his
conception of the moral ideal was, as it is generally
recognised, poles apart from that of the Scribes and
Pharisees. 'Except your righteousness shall exceed the
righteousness of the Scribes and Pharisees ye shall in no
case enter into the Kingdom.' How deep was the cleavage between the two systems of morality is shown by
his treatment of the law of the Sabbath. According to the

[1] *Confessions*, X.6.2.

rabbis a law could be overridden only by another law; but in defending the action of the disciples in eating the ears of corn as they went through the cornfields on the Sabbath day our Lord appealed not to another law but to an historical example, viz. David eating the holy 'bread of the presence', which only the priests were, according to the Law, allowed to eat. This, from the standpoint of the rabbis, was an utterly invalid moral argument. The fact that Christ availed himself of it showed his deep-seated objection to the legalism of the rabbis.

What was the reason for this? The answer to this question brings to light another aspect of the Christian moral ideal which is closely, nay inseparably, bound up with the doctrine of the primacy of love. When we enquire why our Lord wished to overthrow the legalistic morality of the rabbis the answer soon becomes apparent. It is that a code morality leads directly to pride and self-satisfaction. If we have carefully carried out the commands and the rules we can sit back self-satisfied and content. We have done what is required. We then become 'proud' like the Pharisees. But pride and love are completely in opposition. The lover, *qua* lover, is never proud. He is filled with the sense of his unworthiness: he is never good enough for such a girl, she is never good enough for such a man. Thus it is that we are led to what is perhaps the most truly characteristic of all Christian virtues, viz. humility. There is no other creed or system of ethics which exalts the virtue of humility as does Christianity, or indeed really regards it as a virtue at all. Christianity exalts it because in the life of our Lord we see it as the other side of love. It is the gentle shadow cast by love in which the lover is content to slip out of sight. When for love of mankind— 'for us men and for our salvation'—our Lord came down from heaven on Christmas Day his love for man led him to choose a poor and humble lot. He was born in a stable; he lived and worked in a humble home, working at a humble trade. When he went out on his ministry he was to be found with 'the common people' who 'heard him gladly' and even with the outcasts and disreputables. He never thought of himself or stood upon his dignity; and at the last he was content to be mocked and spat upon and nailed to a shameful cross. Ever since then the Christian ideal has been the ideal of love and humility: for this is the true imitation of Christ.

So far we have considered the Christian standard and ideal from the point of view of the individual; but we have to remember that there is also a Christian social ideal which has to be taken into account. It is, indeed, true that for long periods in the history of the Church this has been neglected and sometimes even denied. It has been argued, for example, even in recent times that it is as absurd to talk of a Christian sociology as it would be to talk of a Christian chemistry or physics. It is well known to everybody that at the time of the Industrial Revolution in this country the average Churchman regarded with utter complacency what today we should all regard as great social evils, such as child labour in mines and factories and sweated labour among the very poor. Moreover, as everybody knows, slavery was tolerated by the Church from New Testament times onwards until modern times.

Nevertheless, it is true that from the first the gracious and civilising influence of Christianity began to be felt. How great this was Lecky, who was not himself a Christian, testified in an eloquent passage in his *History of European Morals* which we must quote: 'It is the peculiarity of the Christian types that, while they have fascinated the imagination, they have also purified the heart. The tender, winning, and almost feminine beauty of the Christian Founder, the Virgin Mother, the agonies of Gethsemane or Calvary, the many scenes of compassion and suffering that fill the sacred writings are the pictures which, for eighteen hundred years, have governed the imaginations of the rudest and most ignorant of mankind. Associated with the fondest recollections of childhood, with the music of the church bells, with the clustered lights and the tinsel splendour that seem to the peasant the very ideal of majesty; painted over the altar where he received the companion of his life, around the cemetery where so many whom he had loved were laid, on the stations of the mountain, on the portal of the vineyard, on the chapel where the storm tossed mariner fulfils his grateful vow; keeping guard over his cottage door, and looking down upon his humble bed, forms of tender beauty and gentle pathos for ever haunt the poor man's fancy, and silently win their way into the very depths of his being. More than any spoken eloquence, more than any dogmatic teaching, they transform and subdue his character, till he learns to realise the sanctity of weakness and suffering, the supreme majesty of compassion and weakness. . . . The high conception that has been formed of the sanctity of human life, the protection of infancy, the elevation and final emancipation of the slave classes, the suppression of barbarous games, the creation of a vast and multifarious organisation of charity, and the education of the imagination by the Christian type, constitute together a movement of philanthropy which has never been paralleled or approached in the pagan world.'[1]

It has to be remembered that in the early days of Christianity the Church was a tiny minority in a vast pagan world; and yet, in spite of this, it exerted a remarkable and growing influence, which was, of course, much increased after the persecutions ceased and it was liberated by the accession of Constantine as Roman Emperor.

[1] W. E. H. Lecky: *History of European Morals* (1913), Vol. 2, pp. 99 and 100.

From that time onwards it gradually attained a dominating position, until Christian standards in many matters came to be accepted; particularly in the attitude to money. Usury was strongly condemned and the doctrine of the just price came to be widely accepted. It was not until after the Reformation, as R. H. Tawney showed in his *Religion and the Rise of Capitalism*, that these social moral principles went by the board and an unbridled individualism led the way to an unbridled capitalism, in which money became the god of many to the undoing of society. As a consequence of this, for two hundred years the social aspect of Christianity was almost entirely overlooked by the Church in general and by the Church of England in particular. Speaking of the early part of the nineteenth century the Hammonds could write of 'the feeling that the Church gave its sanction to all the injustices and abuses that degraded the poor and outraged their self-respect'. But this was the darkness before the first streaks of dawn of a renewed Christian conscience, which began with J. M. F. Ludlow, F. D. Maurice and Charles Kingsley—reforming layman, theologian, and country priest respectively. These men it was who enabled the Church of England to begin to see that, in the words of Maurice, 'the will of God should be recognised in all affairs public or private', and to rescue her from slavery to vested interests and an obsolete social and political system. These men and those who thought as they did soon came to be called Christian Socialists, although the latter term was not very clearly defined. Broadly speaking 'Socialism' in this context referred to those men and women who clearly perceived that the Gospel must have a social as well as an individual dimension. Thanks to their efforts such a statement seems to be the merest platitude today, but in the first half of the nineteenth century it was an unheard of idea. That is why for the majority of Churchmen in this country at

that time the theological and sociological implications of
the Industrial Revolution were totally unperceived.

As time went on, these 'new' ideas led to the formation
of various groups and societies within the Church of
England; first the Guild of S. Matthew, then the Christian Social Union and then the Church Socialist League.
As a result the leaven slowly permeated the lump until
what at one time were regarded as dangerous novelties
became commonplaces widely accepted by the faithful.
Thus in 1917, when the celebrated National Mission of
Repentance and Hope was held in this country and
supported by the Church of England as a whole, it
could be said in one of the official documents: 'There is a
real difference between a converted nation and a nation
of converted individuals.' It came to be accepted that
there is and always must be, a social Gospel, and many
came to wonder how anybody could be so blind as to
read the New Testament without seeing this. From the
turn of the nineteenth century and onwards some great
men had proclaimed this in season and out of season:
B. F. Westcott, Henry Scott Holland, Chares Gore and
William Temple, to mention only a few. But how to
work this out in practice was, and still is, no easy matter.
To this day there are still difficult social problems to be
solved, some of them actually caused by the very success
of the early Christian Socialists, who may not unfairly be
called the progenitors of the modern Welfare State which
in turn has created not a few new problems. Moreover,
the problem of raising the 'wage earner' to being in a
real sense a partner in industry has still to be solved. The
monetary system has still to be freed from bondage to
financial abstractions and to be Christianised; the land
and the rural community has still to receive adequate
protection from those who would ruthlessly exploit them.
But the difference today is that there are some at least
in the Church of England who are not unmindful of the

M

fact that such problems as these *are* the concern of the
Church. As a modern writer has said: 'The social movement *in* the Church of England is now in principle, and
in some measure in practice, the social movement *of* the
Church of England.'[1]

The significance of the Cross as the symbol of the
Christian social ideal has, in recent years, often been
pointed out, and it is difficult to think of one which is
more illuminating. It clearly shows the threefold reference which must govern the truly Christian way of
living. First, the Cross points upwards. This indicates the
divine reference which must always direct Christian
living and thinking. Secondly it points sideways, indicating our duty and responsibility as Christians to our
fellow men. Thirdly it points down to the earth in which
it is rooted, thereby revealing the responsibility of the
Christian to reverence the earth and all material things
as belonging to God and so to be used for the glory of
God and not to satisfy the greed of man. It is true to
say that, although unfortunately the average Christian is
very far from clearly perceiving the truth of all this, and
still further from trying to carry it out in practice, there
is at any rate an increasing number of Christians who do
both these things. It is certainly part of the task of the
student of moral theology today to keep these matters
before the minds of those who profess and call themselves
Christians.

This brings us to an important question which must be
answered if we are to understand the meaning of the
Christian social ideal. What does Christian 'love' mean as
between different groups and societies? The answer
must be that, strictly speaking, it is meaningless to tell
groups that they must 'love' one another. Love is a
relationship between persons, and groups of men and
women are not persons. Trade unions are not persons;

---

[1] Maurice B. Reckitt: *Maurice to Temple* (1946), p. 207.

nations are not persons, and, therefore, it is no good telling them that they must settle their differences by loving one another. How, then, according to Christianity, are their relations to be ordered? William Temple rightly said: 'In problems concerning the relations of corporate groups of men, the way of love lies through justice. . . . What the Christian citizen has to do in most of his problems is to dedicate himself in the power of love to the establishment of justice.'[1]

How, then, can the social ideal of the Church be expressed? Certainly not by the 'application' of cut and dried principles, still less of cut and dried social schemes, to solve social problems. Rather the Christian ideal is expressed by the Church being itself—*i.e.* the Body of Christ and the Household of God—thus enabling all its members to be actively Christian in their daily work, offering it to God, and thinking their way Christianly through the many problems which they meet from day to day. In this way they become the light of the world and the salt of the earth. To quote Temple again:'I am convinced that one reason why the Church has counted for comparatively little in the public affairs of recent times is that its spokesmen have talked a great deal too much about love and not nearly enough about justice. Of course it is true that preachers of the Gospel cannot lay too great an emphasis upon love as the supreme gift of God, by receiving which man becomes for the first time capable of the good life which is God's design for him. But though a preacher cannot extol love too highly he may urge its claims irrelevantly.'[2]

What, then, is the Christian social ideal? The answer can be formulated in different ways depending upon the relation of Church and State, provided that the Church has liberty to live her own life and order her own wor-

---

[1] W. Temple: *Citizen and Churchman* (1941), pp. 78 and 79.
[2] *Ibid.*

ship freely. The most obvious way for this to happen is for the Church and the State to be regarded as separate societies[1] but working together in harmony, the former being primarily concerned with the spiritual interests of the citizens, and the latter with their material interests. If all the citizens, however, are at least nominally Christians, as was the case in England in the Middle Ages and at the time of the Reformation, Church and State consist of the same persons regarded merely from different points of view. Whichever way it is, however, Christian social principles must be embodied in the national life. These, broadly speaking, are three. First, there is the principle of the infinite and equal value of all human beings. Therefore the State must not allow individuals to be exploited or regarded as mere tools or 'hands'. Secondly, all men are to be regarded as brothers being children of the one heavenly Father, irrespective of race, class or natural ability. Thirdly, there is the principle of human responsibility, whereby all our human powers and possessions are held in trust from God for the common good.

Within the State, however, there are various societies and groupings the rights of which, embodied in these principles, must be respected. The first and most fundamental of these is the family. According to Christian teaching no State has the right to disrupt or to enslave the family, which is a divine institution for which there is no substitute. Secondly, there are various groups and societies which are formed by those who share a common interest or purpose which they wish to further. Such are trade unions, city companies, schools, colleges and philanthropic societies. Thirdly, there is the Church of God, the Fellowship of the Spirit, which is a divine and not a man-

---

[1] J. N. Figgis, *Churches in the Modern State* (1914), has shown that this has never been explicitly recognised by lawyers. On the one side stands the state; over against it are, not lesser societies, but legal trusts and individuals.

made society, which the State must not try to dominate or enslave, as dictators of all kinds have always tried to do.

The Christian, therefore, cannot tolerate any kind of totalitarian State, whether communist or fascist, because the latter cannot allow any liberty to societies within the State, and forcibly restrains any such groupings. Totalitarianism means the setting up of the kingdom of man and the attempt to cast down the kingdom of God. There are many at this time engaged in this attempt. 'The issue during the next decades in western industrial countries is whether the industrial workers will put their faith in a kingdom of man or the Kingdom of Christ.'[1]

Unfortunately, however, there are still many Christians whose approach to Christianity is far too individualistic. Such, for example, is the Gospel as preached by such a person as Billy Graham, where the social aspect of the Gospel is almost, if not entirely, neglected. The same still holds true of too many middle-aged churchmen and churchwomen who think of religion as a private affair between the soul and God and whose idea of Christian worship is still that of the quiet 'early service'.

The rise of the 'Parish Communion' in the last thirty or forty years—which is one of the most remarkable phenomena in the history of the Church of England, and which has now influenced the Church of Rome—has changed all that. It is now a commonplace to say that the Holy Eucharist embodies in a nutshell the social ideals of Christianity. The Offertory—no longer confused with the alms, by the enlightened churchman—brought up by two or three members of the congregation—is understood to mean the offering of daily life and work to God; bread, the staff of life, being the perfect symbol of that. The Communion is understood more and more to be not only vertical between God and the individual

[1] *Report of the Lambeth Conference* (1948), Part 2, p. 21.

communicant but also horizontal between the communicants themselves. It is, in fact, in the shape of the Cross, and this is costing, and still resisted by some; but there is no doubt that this teaching has come to stay and is having an increasing and powerful influence upon the life of the Church and helping the ordinary churchman to remember that his religion is not just a private matter between his soul and God.

8

The Nature of Anglican
Authority

BISHOP KIRK has said that the Church of England has
spoken mainly by custom and not by law.[1] This testi-
mony is true, despite appearances to the contrary, as we
shall see. It might seem at first sight that it has relied
chiefly upon force and the arm of the State. For example,
in 1662 the Act of Uniformity enforced the Prayer Book
annexed thereto upon the Church, and expelled all who
would not conform. And, prior to that, the measures
by which Ecclesia Anglicana was reformed were acts of
State. But they were not *merely* acts of State. Behind them
lay the mind and conscience of a large body of the
English people. Otherwise these acts of State could not
have ultimately prevailed; for history clearly shows that
acts of State are apt to be ineffective unless they have the
backing of public opinion. A good example of this fact is
afforded by the Prohibition laws in the U.S.A. which
failed dismally because they did not have the necessary
support in the country.

Furthermore, in so far as the authority of the Church of
England has been based upon the Establishment and the
secular arm of the law, this has often been an embarrassment rather than a help to the Church. And this is still

[1] See K. E. Kirk: *Ignorance, Faith and Conformity* (1933), pp. 148ff. Cf. *Conscience
and its Problems* (1st edn.), pp. 86ff.

the case. A good instance is provided by the proposed revised canon on the seal of Confession, clause 5 of which at present runs: 'If any person confesses his secret and hidden sin to a priest for the unburdening of his conscience, and to receive spiritual consolation and absolution from him, such Priest is hereby strictly charged and admonished that he do not at any time reveal and make known to any person whatsoever any sin so committed to his trust and secrecy.' Since, however, owing to the conditions of the Establishment the Canons of the Church of England must receive the Royal Assent and become part of the law of the land, the Crown lawyers are making difficulties over this clause, because, if passed, it would put Church of England priests in a privileged position by giving them legal protection in observing the seal—a privileged position which they do not seek—as (for example) contrasted with their Roman Catholic brethren. Owing to this fact, great pressure was brought to bear on the Convocations to withdraw this clause,[1] or to water it down so that it becomes worthless. Thus here we see how the influence of the authority of the State is endangering the moral and spiritual authority of the Church.

The State element in Anglican authority, as we may describe it, has also led to a weakening of that authority for another reason. The discipline of civil law is commonly exercised not against moral offences *as such* but against crimes and felonies. Consequently it has been widely held that to punish such offences against the Church as heresies and liturgical offences by making them infringements of civil law (because of the Establishment) is unfitting and wrong in principle. Such offences carry no moral stigma, as infringements of civil law commonly do. Consequently when such offences have been punished by

---

[1] Unfortunately this succeeded in October 1966 when the Convocations withdrew the clause.

fines and imprisonment, as in the so-called 'Ritual Prosecutions' in the nineteenth century, this course has failed disastrously, and the Bishops ceased to put the law into operation. The result has been a grave weakening of the authority of the Church of England, which has been described by some as devoid of all discipline, a society without any Rules. This impression has been strengthened by the fact that its canons are 350 years old and are in many cases obsolete through desuetude.

It was to remedy this situation that in 1939 Archbishop Lang of Canterbury and Archbishop Temple of York appointed a Canon Law Commission with the following terms of reference:

A. To consider and report on the questions:
   (1) What is the present status of Canon Law in England (a) as regards Canons in force before the Reformation: (b) as regards Canons made and promulgated since the Reformation? and
   (2) What method should be followed to determine which Canons are to be regarded as obsolete and to provide the Church with a body of Canons certainly operative and apart from which none would be operative or reasonably regarded as operative?
B. To prepare, if after such consideration this seems expedient, a revised body of Canons based on the conclusions reached under A above, for submission to the Convocations.

In 1947 this Commission issued its Report which contained a body of 134 draft canons. This was submitted to the Convocations, and also by the direction of the Presidents submitted to the House of Laity for their consideration, and the lengthy process of revising the draft canons was begun. It now nears completion, but there are still one or two difficult problems to be overcome.

Side by side with the revision of the canon law has gone the effort to reform the Church Courts; for clearly, unless the authority of the latter commends itself to the mind and conscience of the Church any attempt to enforce the canons is doomed to failure. Accordingly in 1951 the two Archbishops appointed another commission to deal with the question of the Reform of the Church Courts with the following terms of reference:

1. To take into review:

    (a) The general system of ecclesiastical courts as set out in draft Canons cxii-cxxv of the Report on the Canon Law of the Church of England, below the Final Court of Appeal, and not including such Final Court.

    (b) The nature of the Laws, statutory or otherwise, administered by the said Courts in so far as they concern charges which may be brought against clerks in holy orders whether on grounds of conduct or of doctrine, ritual, or ceremonial.

    (c) The Church Assembly Measures entitled 'The Incumbents (Discipline) Measure', 'The Church Dignitaries (Retirement) Measure', 'The Bishops (Retirement) Measure'.

    (d) The following Resolution passed by the Church Assembly on 15 November 1949:
    'That the Assembly does not desire that the Bishops (Retirement) Measure (No. 2) shall make provision for the entertainment of complaints against bishops involving questions of doctrine, ritual, and ceremonial; but requests the Convocations to give some priority to the making of such provision in the course of their revision of the Canons and to make it in respect both of the bishops and of the clergy.'

    (e) Any other matters relevant to the above.

2. To report the results of this review and to draw attention to matters which in the opinion of the Commission would justify further action whether by Canon or Measure or Act of Parliament.

In 1954 they issued their Report which in due course was presented to the Church Assembly, where it was debated at length. As a result, *the Ecclesiastical Jurisdiction Measure* was agreed, embodying most, but not all, of the recommendations of the Commission. On 31 July 1963 this measure received the Royal Assent and it is now the law of the land. It did not come before the Convocations *as such*; but since all the members of the four Houses of Convocation are members of the Church Assembly, it is deemed to have received the approval of the former.

The best method of appreciating the significance of the present position is to review briefly the history of canon law in the Church of England and the history of the Church Courts in this land. This we must now do, beginning with the canon law.

Prior to the Reformation the canon law was derived from the ancient customs of the Church and Papal decrees. After the Reformation in the Church of England obviously the latter ceased to be binding *proprio vigore*, although much of this law was also based on long continuing custom and remained in force, as we shall see. But the Papal authority was replaced by the Act of the Submission of the Clergy in 1534. The effect of this Act is summarised in the Report of the Canon Law Commission as follows:

A. Parliament recognised and affirmed the power of the Church to legislate in ecclesiastical matters.

B. Parliament limited and controlled this power by providing:

  1. That the clergy can assemble in convocations only in pursuance of a writ in that behalf received from the Crown.
  2. That they can make canons only with the licence of the Crown.
  3. That canons so made are inoperative unless and until they receive the Royal assent.
  4. That even then they are inoperative if and so far as they offend against the royal prerogative or the Common or Statute Law or the custom of this country.

The two Houses of Parliament, by directing that the Convocations of the Clergy Measure, 1920, should be presented to his Majesty and his Majesty by signifying the Royal Assent thereto gave a modern recognition to the constitutional position above stated.

The Act of 1534 laid it down that canons, constitutions, ordinances and synodals provincial being already made 'which be not contrarient or repugnant to the law, statutes and customs of this realm, nor to the damage or hurt of the King's prerogative' were to continue in force until revised by the Commissioners appointed by the Act, and that this should also apply to 'other ecclesiastical laws or jurisdictions spiritual as be yet accustomed and used here in the Church of England'.

This last clause is of the utmost importance for the understanding of English canon law for it bases the latter on *custom* and not simply on decree or statute or enactment; and those parts of the *Corpus Juris Canonici* which are retained are retained not because they were originally decreed by Papal authority, but because of the authority of long-standing custom in the Church. This is a return to the most ancient principles of canon law before the rise of the Papal power. So, for example, we find them in the famous sixth canon of the Council of Nicaea: 'Let the ancient customs prevail.' Here is the true basis of canon law which, despite the steady growth of Papal power, we still find in Aquinas. He says: 'Custom has the force of law, and abolishes law, and is the interpreter of law',[1] provided of course that it is not contrary to the divine law or the natural law, which also proceeds from God.[2] Aquinas here quotes S. Augustine to the effect that those who throw contempt on the customs of the Church ought to be punished as those who disobey the law of God. This is reasonable, for the Church is the Body of Christ, guided by the Holy Spirit. Consequently widespread custom in the Church, expressing as it does the mind of the Church, may be taken to express also the mind of the Spirit.

Unfortunately this ancient doctrine of canon law as *mos* became assimilated to an entirely different concep-

[1] *Summa Theologica*, Ia IIae Q.97, a.3.   [2] *Ibid.*

tion of law as *lex* as found in Roman civil law. So we find
it in the Code of Justinian, for example: *Quod principi
placuit legis vigorem habet.* This assimilation of canon law as
mos to Civil Law as *lex* was a great misfortune.[1] But
fortunately, as we have seen, the idea of canon law as *mos*
was never completely smothered in the Church of
England. As Hooker says, 'That which hath been received long sithence and is by custom now established,
we keep as a law which we may not transgress.'[2]

Thus the effect of the Tudor legislation was largely to
leave the traditional canon law untouched; but precisely
and in detail what part of the ancient law remained as
before was left unspecified, although obviously those
parts which depended solely upon Papal authority,
unsupported by long-standing custom, went by the
board. In addition, 'The Prayer Book with its prefaces
and rubrics, the various royal and episcopal orders and
injunctions issued in Queen Elizabeth's reign, and the
post-Reformation canons dealing with the conduct of
church services, and church ornaments, took the place
of the few titles which the *Decretals* contained on
matters liturgical, a point on which the ecclesiastical
lawyers were quite definite.'[3] There is nothing revolutionary here, however, for even in pre-Reformation
times certain parts of church life were regulated by
common and statute laws administered in the temporal
courts. But after the Reformation statute law increased its
control in Church affairs, and it now became part of the
law administered in the ecclesiastical courts. For the
judges in the Church courts had now to take into account
any relevant parliamentary statutes, although, until the
nineteenth century, the number of them was small.

A highly important development took place in 1603,
when the Convocations passed a series of 141 new canons,

[1] See above, p. 11.   [2] *Ecclesiastical Polity*, I. 10.8., cf. II 5.7.
[3] *The Canon Law in the Church of England*, p. 47.

of which 97 were adaptations of previous canons, orders and injunctions. 'The code, which grew up to meet the requirements in the administration of the Church during the years succeeding the Reformation, gave definiteness and cohesion to the Church of England in its reformed state. It stated clearly who were, and who were not, members of the Church of England by excommunicating *ipso facto* all who impugned the King's supremacy, the public worship of God established in the Church, the Thirty-Nine Articles, episcopal government, and the Ordinal. It aimed at securing that the clergy who ministered in the Church were loyal to its doctrinal formularies, its liturgy, and its discipline, and at putting an end to the abuses in the ecclesiastical courts which had in the reign of Queen Elizabeth been the cause of much scandal.'[1]

Something must now be said about the Church courts in which this law has been administered. Prior to the Reformation, this was done in a system of four courts. The court of first instance was that of the Archdeacon; from him appeal lay successively to the Bishop, to the Archbishop, and finally to the Pope. After the abolition of the Papal jurisdiction in England, the fourth court of appeal became the High Court of Delegates, which consisted of four judges appointed by the Lord Chancellor separately for each case. A final petition to the Crown from the Court of Delegates was still possible. In practice this procedure was rather loosely followed. In addition, after the Reformation this scheme was modified by the Court of High Commission and also by the system of Peculiars. In a Peculiar the judicial functions of the Archdeacon and the Bishop were exercised either by the Crown, the Archbishop, or the Bishop of another diocese, or, in some cases, by a Dean and chapter, or even an individual member of a chapter or the incumbent of a

[1] *Op. cit.*, p. 74.

parish or lord of the manor. Appeal from a Peculiar
court lay either to the Bishop—in the case of the court of
an incumbent or lord of the manor—or, in other cases, to
the Archbishop.

In 1830 a Royal Commission was appointed to
examine and report on the working of the Church courts,
and, as a result of their findings, in 1835 the appellate
jurisdiction of the Court of Delegates was transferred by
the Privy Council Appeals Act to the Judicial Committee
of the Privy Council. The reasons for this change, which
was to have such unfortunate consequences, were twofold. First, since the composition of the Court of Delegates differed from case to case it was difficult, or impossible, to secure any kind of uniformity in its decisions or
even its rules of procedure, especially as the Court did
not deliver or explain the grounds of its judgements.
Secondly, the composition of the Court was open to
objection, for it consisted of common law judges, unfami-
liar with ecclesiastical law and practice, together with
advocates from Doctors' Commons, who were usually
the more inexperienced members of the profession,
because the senior ones had been already engaged as
counsel when the cases came before the lower courts and
therefore were not eligible as judges of appeal.

The Act of 1832 was followed by a series of Acts of
Parliament which abolished Peculiar courts, and which
transferred matrimonial and testamentary cases to new
secular courts set up for the purpose. As a result of this
legislation a dual system of ecclesiastical courts came into
existence. There was the ancient system of Church
courts modified by Parliamentary statutes, and side by
side with it a system for dealing with cases of clergy discipline. In all this, it should be carefully noted, the influence of the secular law on the Church courts has been
steadily increased. For the substitution of the Judicial
Committee for the Court of Delegates has involved the

inclusion in the canon law of the doctrine of binding precedents, because the Judicial Committee publishes not only its judgements but also the reasons for them. Since these judgements, once they are delivered, become binding also on the lower courts, it will easily be seen how considerable this increased influence of the secular law has been.

This revised system of Church courts has been strongly repugnant to the consciences of many of the clergy and of the laity, being dominated, as it is, by the appellate jurisdiction of the Judicial Committee—a secular body empowered to pass judgement in matters of faith and worship. The objections to this court have been summarised by Archbishop Garbett as follows: 'Those who object to the Judicial Committee as the final court of appeal in ecclesiastical questions would do so on the grounds both of principle and of actual practice. In principle they would say it is wrong for a secular court, however excellent it may be, to declare the law on doctrine or worship. The Church alone, under the guidance of the Holy Spirit, has the right to formulate its doctrine and worship. It has been the tradition of the Church from the Apostolic Age that the Bishops should act for the Church. The Judicial Committee is a secular and not a spiritual court. It was created by the State; it is responsible to the State, and its power depends upon the State. Its judges need be neither churchmen nor even believers. That such a court so constituted should be the final arbitrator on Church doctrine is contrary to the whole conception of the Church as a spiritual, self-governing fellowship, inspired and guided into all truth by the Holy Spirit.'[1]

This opposition came to a head in the nineteenth century in the so-called Ritual Prosecutions in connexion with the Public Worship Regulation Act of 1874. By the

[1] C. F. Garbett: *Church and State in England* (1950), pp. 259, 260.

terms of this Act priests convicted in the Church courts of ritual or ceremonial offences could be sent to prison for a period up to three years if they refused to recant. Not a few, indeed, did pay this extreme penalty, and this led to so great a revulsion of feeling that, after a time, the Bishops refused to put this legal machinery into operation. This, in turn, led to an increasing disregard of the law and to something approaching liturgical chaos. It has all been most damaging to the authority of the Church of England to control its own members, and especially the clergy. Every priest on being admitted to a benefice makes a solemn promise to use the Book of Common Prayer in the conduct of public worship 'and none other, except in so far as it shall be ordered by lawful authority'. But nobody could tell him the exact meaning of the exceptive clause.

It was to rectify this situation that, following upon the revision of the Canons and the findings of a Commission appointed in 1951 to suggest how to reform the Church courts, two measures were brought before the Church Assembly, viz. The Ecclesiastical Jurisdiction Measure, which received the Royal Assent in 1963, and The Prayer Book (Alternative and Other Services) Measure, which received the Royal Assent two years later. It is in the second of these that the present nature of Anglican authority in the sphere of liturgy and worship is most clearly to be seen. In presenting this Measure for final approval in the Church Assembly the Archbishop of Canterbury summarised its purpose and probable effect as follows:

(1) First, it will achieve a very modest and restricted autonomy for the Church in the making of variations and experiments in public worship. I would emphasise how very modest these powers will be. The Cecil Commission on Church and State in 1935 urged the need for considerably greater autonomy. There have been eminent churchmen, notably Archbishop

N

Garbett and Bishop George Bell, who regretted that the more radical course then proposed was not pursued at the end of the War. But the present proposals are based upon the findings of the Moberly Commission in 1952, and these findings were endorsed in principle by this Assembly. I believe that it is a prerequisite for any larger autonomy within the Establishment that there should be Synodical Government with the laity integrated with the clergy and the Bishops in the direction of the Church, and that the Church should use the modest powers of experiment under this Measure with unity of purpose.

(2) Second, the Measure provides a clear interpretation of the meaning of the words 'Lawful authority' in the declaration made by the priest and the deacon at ordination and by the priest on his institution to a benefice when he promises 'to use the form in the said book prescribed and none other except so far as shall be ordered by lawful authority'.

The interpretation is not a narrow one. It includes services authorised for experimental use under this Measure. It includes, for occasions other than those of the Prayer Book, services authorised by the Convocations, by the ordinary and in some cases by the parish priest all under various controlling safeguards. But the definition is, though not narrow, perfectly clear. And the interpretation will remove an uncertainty which has been most distressing. I remember, after my own ordination when I had made the declaration, the Bishop suddenly said to me 'and what do you understand lawful authority to mean?' I said 'I think it means so and so', and the Bishop did not rebuke me for my ignorance and uncertainty but said in a kindly voice 'Yes, I think it means that, but we are not quite sure'. It is very unsatisfactory to say the least that the meaning of so solemn a declaration should be uncertain to him who makes it and to him who administers it.

According to the provisions of this Act, as it has now become, it is permitted to make use of experimental forms of service for a period of seven years, renewable for another period of seven years, provided that such forms pass the Houses of Convocation and the House of Laity in the Church Assembly, after obtaining a two-thirds majority in each House. It is also allowable for forms of

service for special occasions to be used and for the parish
priest to 'make and use variations which are not of
substantial importance' in any form of service prescribed
by the Book of Common Prayer or authorised for use
under this Measure according to particular circumstances.

Two points of especial importance about this new
Measure should be noted. In the first place, the parish
priest is allowed liberty to make 'minor variations' in the
prescribed forms of service. Hitherto he has had no such
liberty but was bound by law (the authority of which he
did not always recognise) not to deviate from the directions in the Prayer Book by an iota. This is, beyond
question, a reasonable new provision, but it may well lead
to difficulties, as we shall see in a moment.

In the second place, the laity of the Church of England,
as such, are for the first time given the power of veto in
matters of doctrine and worship. Laymen have had this
power hitherto as members of Parliament, a power which
some will think has been abused, as well as wrong
in principle, but they have never possessed it as lay
members of the Church, and this raises important
questions which are not always faced, and, as I think,
have not been fully faced by those who have been
mainly responsible for giving them this power, which is,
comparatively speaking, a novelty in the history of the
Church.

Whether or not these provisions will provide a practical solution of the problems of liturgical authority time
alone can show. So far the omens are not altogether
bright. Thus the 1928 rite of Confirmation which has
been widely used and approved for nearly twenty years
in this country has failed to receive the required two-
thirds majority in the House of Laity: and the Bishops
have had to discontinue its use. Again, the delicately
balanced Eucharistic prayer in the new, Series 2, Holy

Communion service, after passing the Convocations, has been altered at the instance of the House of Laity, thereby rendering it unacceptable to many of the clergy. Yet again, the House of Laity have vetoed the new Burial Office, making suggestions for watering-down the prayers for the departed, and these suggestions have been rejected by both the Convocations. The present position here is deadlock.

We must now pass from the question of Anglican authority in matters of Liturgy to that of Anglican authority in matters of morals. Here there is a wider measure of uncertainty. The competent bodies to provide this authority are the Convocations but apart from the new marriage canons and the Acts of Convocation[1] regulating marriage discipline they have provided less moral guidance than might have been expected concerning the burning moral problems of the day. However, during the past twenty years the following moral issues have been debated in the Church Assembly: The colour bar, betting and gambling, the sale of contraceptives, the Christian and Freemasonry, world hunger, nuclear warfare and abortion. These debates make interesting reading but they do not provide clear moral guidance on these questions. Over the same period of time the Convocation of Canterbury has discussed the race problem more than once, nuclear warfare more than once, nullity of marriage, the moral and spiritual significance of modern scientific discoveries, the rule of law in international relations, and capital punishment.

There is one other source, however, to which the Anglican can look for moral guidance and that is the Reports of the Lambeth Conferences. These, indeed, have no strictly canonical authority but they do nevertheless possess a weighty moral authority which the

[1] See Additional Note on the authority of Convocation on p. 215.

Anglican moral theologian must take into account. Thus in the last fifty years the Lambeth Conferences have made pronouncements on three pressing moral questions: marriage problems, the Race Problem and thermonuclear weapons. It is highly significant that every one of the last four Conferences has issued a statement concerning the moral problems of marriage. Assuredly these are among the most urgent moral problems of the day, and it will help us to appreciate the nature of the Anglican approach to moral theology if we proceed to examine briefly these several statements, although something has already been said on this matter.

We begin with Resolutions 67 and 68 of the 1920 Conference. These run as follows:

67. The Conference affirms as our Lord's principle and standard of marriage a life-long and indissoluble union, for better for worse, of one man with one woman, to the exclusion of all others on either side, and calls on all Christian people to maintain and bear witness to this standard.

Nevertheless, the Conference admits the right of a national or regional church within our Communion to deal with cases which fall within the exception mentioned in the record of our Lord's words in St. Matthew's Gospel, under provisions which such Church may lay down.

The Conference, while fully recognising the extreme difficulty of governments in framing marriage laws for citizens many of whom do not accept the Christian standard, expresses its firm belief that in every country the Church should be free to bear witness to that standard through its powers of administration and discipline exercised in relation to its own members.

68. The Conference, while declining to lay down rules which will meet the needs of every abnormal case regards with grave concern the spread in modern society of theories and practices hostile to the family. We utter an emphatic warning against the use of unnatural means for the avoidance of conception, together with the grave dangers—physical, moral and religious —thereby incurred, and against the evils with which the extension of such use threatens the race. In opposition to the

teaching which, under the name of science and religion, encourages married people in the deliberate cultivation of sexual union as an end in itself, we steadfastly uphold what must always be regarded as the governing consideration of Christian marriage. One is the primary purpose for which marriage exists, namely the continuation of the race through the gift and heritage of children; the other is the paramount importance in married life of deliberate and thoughtful self-control.

We desire solemnly to commend what we have said to Christian people and to all who will hear.

We notice in this statement a pronouncement on two basic questions, which we shall find arising in all succeeding Lambeth Conferences. The first of these is the essential nature of marriage as the indissoluble union of one man with one woman until death; but alongside this there is a reference to the so-called 'Matthaean exception' which allows divorce for the solitary reason of adultery. The basis of this standard is clearly the Holy Scriptures of the New Testament. In the second place, it is stated without qualification that the 'primary purpose for which marriage exists is the continuation of the race through the gift and heritage of children'.

The other basic question on which a pronouncement is made is that of the use of contraceptives, which are condemned without qualification. Clearly no scriptural authority can be directly invoked for this. The condemnation is simply based on the ground that they are 'unnatural' means. In this the Lambeth Fathers are in line with the traditional teaching of the Church.

Passing on to the Conference of 1930 we find a reaffirmation of Resolution 67 of the 1920 Conference which states 'as our Lord's principle and standard of marriage, a life-long and indissoluble union, for better, for worse, of one man with one woman, to the exclusion of all others on either side'. But it is significant that no reference is made to the possible 'Matthaean exception' which allows divorce on the ground of *porneia* alone. This is doubtless due to the fact that during the intervening ten years New Testament scholarship had hardened against the authority of the words in S. Matthew, it being almost universally agreed that they are a later and unauthentic insertion into the earlier text of S. Mark, 10.1–8. Again, scholars were finding it far from easy to be sure of the exact meaning of *porneia* in the text of S. Matthew. This further weakened the evidential value of the 'Matthaean exception'. In so far, therefore, as there is any change here from the 1920 Resolution it is a change in the direction of a greater strictness in the description of the marriage bond.

When, however, we turn to the question of contraception we find the wind of change beginning to blow strongly in favour of relaxing the condemnatory judgements of 1920. In the famous Resolution 15, passed by a two-thirds majority, albeit with a minority of 67 we read: 'When there is a clearly felt moral obligation to limit or to avoid parenthood, the method must be decided on Christian principles. The primary and obvious method is complete abstinence from intercourse (as far as may be necessary) in the life of discipline and self-control lived in the power of the Holy Spirit. Nevertheless in the cases where there is such a clearly-felt obligation to limit or avoid parenthood, and where there is a morally sound reason for avoiding complete abstinence, the Conference agrees that other methods may be used, provided that this is done in the light of the same Christian principles. The Conference records its strong condemnation of the use of any methods of conception control from motives of selfishness, luxury or mere convenience'. There follows the brief Resolution 16 which states: 'The Conference further records its abhorrence of the sinful practice of abortion'.

Here we see a definite statement allowing in certain

circumstances that contraceptives may be used. These circumstances may be listed as follows: (a) When there is 'a felt moral obligation to limit or avoid parenthood', and (b) when there is 'a morally sound reason for avoiding complete abstinence'. But no indication is given as to any criteria by which 'moral obligation' or 'a morally sound reason' can be evaluated. We are told, indeed, that the *method* of contraception must be decided 'on Christian principles' but, once again, we are not told which Christian principles.

Thus, so far, we have to criticise this judgement on the ground of vagueness; but there is one sentence in the Resolution which does a good deal to clarify the moral theology on which it is based. It is the sentence in which it is said that 'The primary and obvious method (of conception control) is complete abstinence from intercourse (as far as may be necessary).' The word 'primary' here must surely mean 'primary' in the moral sense; otherwise it is without any clear meaning. If this is the case, it follows that other methods of conception control are morally secondary; and from that it seems to follow that the use of contraceptives when employed conscientiously by a Christian, although permissible, must be adjudged as the lesser of two evils—a lesser evil, in fact, than taking the risk of bringing unwanted children into the world, on one hand, or of over-straining the husband and wife relationship by over-abstinence, on the other. This principle of following the lesser evil is, as we have seen, a perfectly reputable moral principle. It is important to perceive that this crucially important Resolution is, in fact, based upon it.

Owing to the war there follows an interval of 18 years before the next Lambeth Conference (1948) and this reveals a certain weakening of the idea of 'indissolubility' and also a return to the 'Matthaean exception'. The actual Resolution 92 which concerns the basic nature of marriage is somewhat vague. In order to elucidate its meaning, therefore, we must have recourse to the report of the sub-committee dealing with the Church's Discipline in Marriage. The Resolution in question runs:[1] 'Faced with the great increase in the number of broken marriages and the tragedy of children deprived of true home life, this Conference desires again to affirm that marriage always entails a life-long union and obligation: it is convinced that upon the faithful observance of this divine law depend the stability of home life, the welfare and happiness of children, and the real health of society.' In this statement, as contrasted with that of the 1930 Conference, which has already been quoted, it will be observed that the all-important word 'indissoluble' has been omitted. The reason for this becomes clear in the report of the Sub-Committee where a difference of opinion as to the meaning of this term (which appears both in the 1920 and the 1930 Resolutions) is asserted to exist. One view takes 'indissoluble' to mean what it must grammatically mean, viz. 'cannot be dissolved'—the traditional meaning of the word here in western Christendom. The other view, fortified by the doctrine of the Matthaean exception—once more invoked—takes it only to mean 'ought not to be dissolved'. The Sub-Committee rather weakly says: 'We are bound to admit that a union which is indissoluble by divine institution may in fact be wrecked by sin, and that by the sin of one or both the partners the personal relationship in marriage can be completely destroyed.' It must, however, be borne in mind that this strange view of the meaning of the word 'indissoluble' must not be attributed to the Conference as a whole. It is difficult to see how it can be defended. 'Indissoluble' really cannot be made to mean 'ought not to be dissolved.'

We now come to the Report of the most recent

[1] *Ibid.*, p. 98.

Lambeth Conference, that of 1958. In the Resolutions there is no account or reaffirmation of the nature and essence of marriage, as there was in each of the three preceding Conferences. Nor is this deficiency really made good in the Report where we find the phrase 'human sexuality' when we should expect to find the word 'marriage'. Thus we read: 'Three purposes—three functions—are interwoven in human sexuality. Each of them is profoundly rooted in human experience and in God's revelation. The procreation of children, the fulfilment and completion of husband and wife in each other, and the establishment of a stable environment within which the deepest truths about human relationships can be expressed and communicated and children grow up.'[1] The obvious and more accurate word to use here would surely have been 'marriage'; for sexuality as such does not lead directly to the formation of 'a stable environment'. Again, the expressions 'family life' or 'the family' are often used when we should have expected the word 'marriage'. And there is great hesitation about the use of the word 'indissolubility' in this connexion when speaking of the 'permanence' of family ties. We read: 'This is not to idealise "indissolubility" alone, which, if it is not accompanied by the other necessities of true family life, can poison and destroy.'[2] And the writers go on to conclude: 'A man may be a bad brother or an unworthy son, but brother and son he is, regardless of whether he lives up to it or not.' That is precisely what is meant, *mutatis mutandis*, by saying of husband and wife that they are joined together indissolubly. There seems here to be some confusion of thought.

Turning to the question of contraception, this is without qualification commended in Resolution 115 which reads: 'The Conference believes that the responsibility for deciding upon the number and frequency of children

[1] Report of 1958 Lambeth Conference, p. 144.   [2] *Ibid.*, p. 150.

has been laid by God upon the consciences of parents everywhere; that this planning (the first appearance of this question-begging term), in such ways as are mutually acceptable to husband and wife in Christian conscience, is a right and important factor in Christian family life and should be the result of positive choice before God. Such responsible parenthood, built on obedience to all the duties of marriage, requires a wise stewardship of the resources and abilities of the family as well as a thoughtful consideration of the varying population needs and problems of society and the claims of future generations'.

Here we see a unanimous approval of the use of contraceptives on two conditions: (a) Agreement of husband and wife and (b) 'In Christian conscience'—a vague expression which affords no detailed guidance.

In the 1958 Conference Report of the Sub-Committee on the Family in Contemporary Society four other relevant moral issues are mentioned: Pre-marital intercourse, abortion, artificial insemination and sterilisation.

As for pre-marital intercourse, this is condemned on the ground that it is incompatible with the 'full giving and receiving of the whole person which sexual intercourse expresses'.[1] Abortion is condemned without qualification as being infanticide, as in the case of previous Conferences.

The last two moral problems appear in a Lambeth Conference Report for the first time. These both receive a qualified approval: artificial insemination in the case of the husband's semen only, and sterilisation only if it is voluntary and even then only for stringent medical reasons—e.g. to remove a malignant growth.

We may now briefly survey the moral principles underlying these Lambeth Conference pronouncements. In the first place, we notice the reliance on the authority

[1] *Ibid.*, p. 156.

of Holy Scripture where it is available. This is entirely in accordance with the Anglican tradition. Thus we find in 1920 a loophole of escape from the strict doctrine of the indissoluble nature of marriage on the basis of the 'Matthaean exception'. But in 1930 this bolt-hole is closed because Biblical scholarship in the intervening ten years had done much to undermine the authority of the first Evangelist as a witness to our Lord's teaching.

In 1948 we observe a definite weakening of belief in the indissolubility of marriage, but the only argument in support of this weakening is an appeal to the alleged ambiguity of the word 'indissoluble'—surely an unsatisfactory argument which cannot be sustained. The real ground of the weakened doctrine of marriage which is entertained would seem to be the corroding influence of public opinion. To say as the Report does that 'a union which is indissoluble by divine institution may in fact be wrecked by sin' is to assent to a contradiction.

In 1958, most surprisingly, nothing at all is said about the essential nature of marriage. It is hard to know what to make of this. Whatever the reason, the position here is far from satisfactory; for the need for a clear statement was by no means diminished in 1958.

The other moral problems involved in marriage unfortunately cannot be directly solved by an appeal to the Scriptures, for the simple reason that the latter have nothing to say about them. The most pressing of these is undoubtedly that of the use of contraceptives. Here we notice a significant change in the various pronouncements. In the first of these four Conferences they are condemned out of hand as being 'unnatural' thus following the ancient tradition of the Church. In 1930 they are still condemned by a substantial minority of the Bishops, but given a qualified approval by the majority, on the ground that to use them may be better in some circumstances than not to do so—an appeal to the

Aristotelian principle that in the case of a choice of evils we should choose the lesser.

When we come to 1948 it is disappointing that the Conference remains silent on the question of contraception. Nor is anything, as might have been expected, said about abortion.

In 1958 the use of contraceptives is approved without qualification provided that they are 'admissible to the Christian conscience'. But no indication is given as to what principles are to be followed by the Christian conscience in forming its judgement. Some methods of conception control which are deemed to be unacceptable to the Christian are, indeed, mentioned—viz. denial of intercourse by one of the parties to the other, and any means 'which interrupts or prevents the fulfilment of coitus'; but even here the reasons are not given. Presumably the former practice is ruled out simply as an act of selfishness; but on what 'Christian' grounds is the latter excluded? Medically, *coitus interruptus* is known to be harmful, but we are not told what exactly are the Christian principles involved in this judgement. Abortion as a means of 'family planning' is condemned out of hand as being 'infanticide'. Sterilisation is condemned as being 'a major and irrevocable abdication of an important area of responsible freedom'. Yet when all this is weighed up the Christian conscience may well feel that it has received what is, to say the least, inadequate guidance when faced by doubt in this important matter. The 1930 Conference majority report made the use of artificial methods of contraception wrong because unnatural, but allowed that this might well be the lesser of two evils—a perfectly intelligible and morally sound moral principle. The 1958 Conference fails in the last resort to give any secure moral guidance at all to the doubtful conscience in this matter.

Turning to the basic nature of marriage—which for

some strange reason is treated after 'family planning'—
we find, once again, a hesitating judgement. We are told
that the marriage relationship is 'permanent'; but we
are also informed: 'This is not to idealise "indissolubility"
alone, in the legal sense, which, if it is not accompanied
by the other necessities of the family life, can poison and
destroy. It is rather to say that the relationships of
husband and wife and children to and among each other
are *given* relationships. A man may be a bad brother or
an unworthy son, but brother and son he is, regardless of
whether he lives up to it or not.' Yet if this argument is
applied to husband and wife once lawfully joined together in marriage, what is this but a statement of
'indissolubility'?

Surveying the ethical significance of the several judgements of these four Lambeth Conferences on the problem
of marriage as indicative of the nature of Anglican moral
authority, what do we find? First, we find, as we should
expect, reliance on the authority of Holy Scripture,
where it is available. Secondly, we find a certain sensi-
tiveness to the movement of contemporary public opinion,
and a readiness to modify moral judgements accordingly.
This is seen notably in the marked change which took
place in the nearly forty years between the Conferences
of 1920 and 1958. The former condemned the practice
of artificial contraception in accordance with the traditional view of the Western Church that it is 'unnatural'.
The latter takes its legitimacy for granted provided that
these methods are used in accordance with 'Christian
conscience' as a serious exercise in human and marital
responsibility.

This position, as we have argued, is not entirely satisfactory. More guidance could and should have been
given to the Christian conscience in this matter, as we
have said. Nevertheless, one is bound to admit that the
position taken in this matter by the Lambeth Fathers—

or to be precise those of them who signed the Report specifically concerned with this matter—is far more satisfactory than that in which the Roman Catholic Church is placed in this matter. Despite the doubts and hesitancies of moral authority as it is understood by Anglicans, the latter are really in a morally sounder position than their Roman Catholic brethren.

When all has been said on the subject of Anglican authority in the matter of morals, there will probably be fairly wide-spread agreement with Bishop Kirk when he said: 'The Church of England has admittedly left her children far too long without adequate guidance in the many intricacies of morality; but she cannot repair the damage in a day. A careful sifting of the conscientious judgements of Christians of every generation and every state of life . . . is urgently necessary before she can set before her members a detailed moral code adequate to their needs.'[1] If, however, what we have written in this book is a true assessment of the position of the Anglican moral theologian, it is doubtful, to say the least, if a 'detailed moral code' is desirable, let alone possible, from the Anglican point of view.

[1] K. E. Kirk: *Conscience and its Problems* (1927), p. 98.

9

The Moral Theologian in a post-Christian Society

IN CONCLUSION, we have now to consider the actual situation in which the moral theologian finds himself today. By 'moral theologian' I mean, of course, not simply the professed teacher of moral theology in a college or a university, but also any man or woman who wishes to follow Christ in the modern world. As we have already noticed, one of the distinctive marks of moral theology as the Anglican sees it is that it seeks to render every man capable of being his own moral theologian. He is therefore in a favourable position to deal with the modern situation, which need not disconcert him. He does not approach it with a cast-iron framework of morals into which he wishes to force everybody. His position is *per se* flexible and adaptable.

We must, however, first of all examine the present moral situation carefully in order to understand it as clearly as possible. It is commonly said that we live in a post-Christian society. By this it is intended to indicate that society is no longer Christian and no longer accepts Christian presuppositions as our forefathers in this land did: and that is true. It could, however, also with equal propriety, be called a post-Darwinian and post-Freudian society; for it is mainly due to the mental earthquakes for which Darwin and Freud were responsible that society has been shaken to its foundations, and the landscape has been reduced to the moral chaos which is the modern world in which multitudes are groping their way.

These devastating changes may be said to have begun in 1859 when Charles Darwin published the *Origin of Species*. In his doctrine of natural selection Darwin sought to show that man is not made in the image of God, as the Scriptures declared, but that, as one Psalmist said, he is like unto the beasts that perish. There is, Darwin thought, no *essential* difference between man and the beasts. He has a larger brain and more intelligence; that is all. He is certainly not, as the Bible teaches, a 'fallen' being. If he has fallen at all, it has been a fall upwards, by which he has gained ever increasing knowledge. Man's primary task, therefore, is to continue his upward progress, outgrowing the tiger and the ape, and more and more increasing his power over nature.

> 'Glory to Man in the highest, for Man is the
> master of things.'[1]

This attitude of mind has been strongly reinforced since 1859 by the astonishing development of modern science, especially of technological science, by which man's domination over nature has grown almost beyond belief. It is true that two world wars have done something to shake man's belief in himself; nevertheless, for many there can be no going back to the pre-Darwinian belief that man is essentially different from all other creatures, being made to reflect the Creator, as no others can.

Moreover, the influence of Darwin has been powerfully reflected in Marxism. In his economic determinism, Karl Marx was strongly influenced by Darwin's teaching. On this question Lord Lindsay wrote: 'Variations

[1] A. C. Swinburne, *Hymn of Man*.

in the means of production brought about by new inventions correspond in Marx to the biological variations in Darwin. As new biological variations cut out the less efficient in the struggle for food, so variations in production cut out by economic competition the older less efficient forms. The prevailing means of production produces its own type of economic structure and division of society into classes. These produce prevailing moral and social opinions which seem to determine and shape the structure of society but are really the effects and not the cause of that structure. The inventions are really as blind as the biological variations, for they are produced with no reference to or prescience of the social results which they produce. Both theories purport to show how a struggle which is itself blind and haphazard produces results which seem purposive because in the process the unfit variations are cut out. For Marx, then, Hegel's dialectic, when it is "put right side up" becomes the materialist conception of history or economic determinism."[1]

The ultimate effect of Darwin's teaching, therefore, has been to create for many millions of people an entirely materialistic background for life, which has made it almost impossibly hard for many of them to accept any ultimate authority in morals, including, of course, Christian morality.

On top of this shattering earthquake, half a century later there came another, introduced by another man of genius, Sigmund Freud. By uncovering the nature of the unconscious mind, Freud showed that it is no longer possible to take human thinking at its face value. We are not always what we appear to be. We are at the mercy of unconscious wishes and desires which can falsify our thinking and make it impossible to discover the Truth, with a capital T. Indeed, said Freud, there is no such Truth to be discovered. Everything, including morality,

[1] A. D. Lindsay: *Karl Marx's Capital* (1947), p. 22.

is relative, simply the result of the interplay of human wishes. Freud's discovery of the unconscious did not necessarily carry with it this deterministic conclusion; but Freud nevertheless drew it, as we saw in a previous chapter. In so doing, he was undoubtedly influenced by his early experiences as a member of the persecuted and hated Jewish people. Indeed, his upbringing was such that he must have been the slave of numerous inhibitions which perverted his thinking.[1] It is one of the curiosities of history, moreover, that the father of psychoanalysis, by which repressions are revealed and liberated, never himself submitted to analysis. If he had done so, he might well have refrained from attaching his rebel materialistic philosophy to his scientific psychology. In fact, he has reinforced the materialistic background formed by Darwinism.

The world in which we have to live today is, in large measure, due to the influence of these two men. There are, of course, many other influences which have been at work,[2] but I would submit that these have been the most fundamental and far reaching, and the effect of them in the field of morality and human conduct has been to turn it into a quagmire, where at times it seems to be impossible to find a sure foothold. Some would say that Freud has turned it into a cesspool.

What has the Christian moralist to say to all this? Of course, if man *is* simply as the beasts that perish, with no hope of immortality, and if human freedom is, as Freud thought, an illusion, *cadit quaestio*; the moral theologian is wasting his time. In that case there is no such thing as virtue, and no such thing as sin, and the most reasonable creed to hold would seem to be contained in the ancient slogan: 'Let us eat and drink, for tomorrow we die.'

---

[1] See H. L. Philp: *Sigmund Freud* (1960) *passim*.
[2] The atheistic influence of the so-called linguistic philosophy, made available to the masses by broadcasting, is specially worthy of note.

O*

The evidence is clear, however, that, Christianity apart, men and women today are not satisfied with this creed. They feel 'in their bones' that it is not the whole truth about human life; and one of the most significant signs of the times is the revival of the great non-Christian religions, revived, as the Christian notes with interest, with not a few Christian characteristics appended. The moral theologian, therefore, need not despair. He does not have to throw in his hand. But what attitude is he to adopt towards the present situation?

One way to deal with it is to take the line of those who advocate what is known as 'the new morality'. This is to reject authority in morals in all its forms and to say that there are no binding moral rules or principles or laws. There is only the actual concrete situation in all its particularity.[1] This leads to existentialism in ethics or to what Joseph Fletcher has called 'situational ethics'. One of the most lucid exponents of this teaching is H. A. Williams. He writes; 'Some people will tell you that the kingdom consists in obedience to a traditional system of ethics. Do this and don't do that, and yours is the kingdom. Obedience of this kind looks like a virtue. In fact, it is always a blasphemy. A blasphemy against oneself. To base and regulate one's life upon other people's rules—even when they call them God's law—this is blasphemous because it is to choose slavery when you could be free. Freedom involves the discovery by each of us of the law of his own being: how he, as a unique person, can express sincerely and fearlessly what he is.'[2] Again, 'The age in which we live is intensely aware of the duty to seek and find the self. Its suspicion of authority, its criticism of established criteria, its art forms, are all a response to what is felt to be life's major moral challenge—how to discover and be what I am. In these

---

[1] J. A. T. Robinson: *Honest to God* (1963), p. 114.
[2] H. A. Williams: *The True Wilderness* (1965), p. 52.

circumstances to preach Christ as he who demands un-qualified submission to another, human or divine, is to confront the world not with Christ but with Judas Iscariot.'[1]

Thus the new moralist would simplify the task of the moral theologian by abolishing the need for the consideration of virtues or sins or casuistry thus reducing the field of moral theology to very slender proportions indeed. All that is required (we are told) is that each individual should be taught how to be himself, freed as far as possible from all inhibitions.

Thus the chaotic situation in which morality is placed today which, as we have seen, is mainly the result of the teaching of two men who were atheists, is to be turned to the glory of the God whom they denied. We are told that the Christian can welcome this situation just because the Christian ethic is an ethic of love, and love dispenses with all laws and principles. To love one's neighbour as oneself, one must first of all be oneself, and then one will see the rightness of according the same privilege to him. Thus also one will love God, who is the ground of the being both of my neighbour and myself.

This all sounds delightfully simple, and it certainly absolves the moral theologian from many of his tasks, but when this position is carefully examined it is seen to be far from satisfactory, because it never comes to grips with the all-important question: What is meant by the 'self'? In his interesting essay in *Soundings* entitled *Theology and Self-awareness* Mr. Williams talks about 'the unknown self' which has to be realised in contrast with the conscious self, which (he says) is commonly the only part of the self taken into consideration when one reflects upon one's conduct; but he fails to show what is the relation between these two 'selves'. To speak of an 'unconscious self' is only a *façon de parler*. In strictness, according to Christian teaching, there is only one self, which is the

[1] *Ibid.*, p. 156.

ego, who is conscious of himself or herself as an individual person.[1] This ego is all the time subject to influences of various kinds. Of some of these he is aware; of others he is not aware; and it has been shown by Freud and others that the latter are quite as important as the former, perhaps more important. Christian theologians, however, have always been fully aware of this and have spoken of the *apex mentis*, or fine point of the soul, as the most direct meeting place between God and man. But this does not mean that the moral life of man is fulfilled simply by giving expression to any and all influences from the unconscious. Some of them, as they impinge on the human soul or personality, are good, but some of them are evil, and the new morality really does nothing to enable us to distinguish with any degree of certainty between the two. Of course the new moralist can say, and does say, to the questioner: it is right and good to follow the path of love. But if the questioner asks why should I, if I don't want to do so? he is in a worse position than the traditional moralist, who would reply: Because it is the will of God who made you after the pattern of his own being.

The truth of the matter is that the new morality is as vague as to the nature of human personality as it is vague as to the nature of Divine personality. More than one writer has pointed out that this is what commonly happens. A weak grasp on the nature of Personality in God is always correlated with a weak grasp of the nature of human personality. In other words, the new morality, like the new theology, has more than a tinge of pantheism in it; and pantheism is 'polite atheism' and ultimately must lead to the obliteration of all moral values.

---

[1] It is not incumbent on the moral theologian to establish the existence of the ego or human soul, whichever term is preferred, any more than it is his business to establish the existence of a personal God. These are, for him, legitimate presuppositions. It is for the dogmatic theologian to establish them. On the existence of the ego Butler's *Dissertation on Personal Identity* has never been refuted.

How, then, are we to explain the amazing popularity of this 'new' approach to the problems of religion and morality? I suggest that at least part of the explanation is that it appeals to the neurotic tendency in the human mind which leads it to suppose that it is possible to have your cake and eat it. Every psychiatrist is only too familiar with the manifestation of this trait in his patients. The new theology, and the morality which goes with it, exemplifies this perfectly. It says, in effect: This is how you can believe in Christianity without really having to believe in God. It is significant that a number of those who took part in *The Honest to God Debate* said something very much like that. Yet, in fact, it is not possible; and it is vital that we should clearly recognise this, if we do not wish to live in a fool's paradise. The 'death of God' theology, which stems from Nietzsche, who ended in a madhouse, is a still less satisfactory attempt to save something from the wreck.

Any such way out of the prevailing moral confusion is a *cul de sac*, a dead-end. We cannot evade in this way the need for a moral standard. However we may twist and turn and seek to evade the issue, we must in the last resort find a secure moral foothold outside ourselves or perish. It is not enough to tell a person to express himself or to be himself. He has also the task of becoming a self worth expressing. What too many of the new moralists fail to recognise is that something has gone radically wrong with mankind, in consequence of which man is a disappointing being. He continually fails to fulfil his promise. G. K. Chesterton put the matter in his inimitable way when he said that the essential difference between man and the lower animals is that, whereas one can slap one's timid friend on the back and say: 'Come on, now, be a man', one would never think of hitting a frightened ape on the back, saying: 'Come on, now, be a monkey'.

In a word, man has a fatal egocentric bias, as we saw in dealing with original sin, and this invalidates the gospel of self-expression. Man is a sinner, and he will find no redemption in himself, any more than he can lift himself by tugging at his own shoe laces. Only God can say: 'I am what I am.' Man, alas, must always say: 'I am not what I am': and God alone can make him to be so.

My submission, then, is that the so-called new morality cannot provide a way out of the prevailing moral confusion in a post-Christian society. There is, however, as I think, another and a better way of meeting the present-day challenge for self-expression and rebellion against authority, and that is by substituting for the spirit of man the Holy Spirit of God. This, however, can be done only if it is clearly understood that a clear-cut distinction must be made between God and man, between the Creator and the creature; in a word, between God and me. Because God influences me at the unconscious level as well as at the conscious level this does not at all mean that the unconscious part of my ego or personality *is* divine. It is just as much a creature as the conscious part is. Consequently it is not enough to try to solve the problem of conduct by telling people that they have only to express themselves freely, without any interference from outside authority and all will be well. Self-expression, if it is to be true self-expression, involves self-surrender. Apart from the question of man's egocentric bias, it would involve that, because man is a creature made to reflect the glory of God. That is what the Bible means when it says that he is made in the image of God. But owing to man's nature being perverted by sin, this process of self-surrender, instead of, so to say, coming automatically and easily, is often hard and painful. Nevertheless, man must live to a centre outside himself if he is to find happiness. That seems to me, at least, to be one of the most luminously clear facts of human experience. The essence of Christian teaching here is to say that this centre must be our Lord Jesus Christ. 'I live, yet not I, but Christ liveth in me' (Gal. 2.20). This is not 'Christ-mysticism'; it is something which every dedicated Christian knows from experience to be true. There is nothing specifically 'mystical' about it.

Two questions arise from what has just been said. The first is the question as to exactly what this surrender involves in relation to moral principles and laws. The second is the practical question as to how this surrender can be achieved.

Turning to the first question, we must begin by considering briefly the psychological development of the human infant from the moment of birth up to the end of the second year or so. The human child is utterly weak, helpless and dependent not simply for hours or days or even weeks, but—in contrast with all other species—for months and even years. Its first requirement is a sense of security and acceptance. This must be derived from the mother or the mother-surrogate. The infant fresh from the adventure of birth (which may have been an unpleasant adventure) urgently needs security. The pattern of this early psychological development can be studied in any text book of psychiatry. It will be convenient to quote the summary which Dr. Frank Lake gives in his *Clinical Theology*. He postulates four phases of development. 'Phase 1. The genesis of Being in Acceptance. The dynamics of the origin of an "I myself". Human personal Being arises in a relationship between an attentive mother and a responsive baby. This constitutes the *way in* to normal dependency. A baby lives in the light of her countenance. This is an obligatory need. Its denial or undue delay leads to an Anxiety of Separation from Being itself. Phase 2. The fulfilment of *Well-Being* by the mother's abundant self-giving, i.e. Sustenance on all levels of life. Phase 3. Dawn of joyful self-consciousness. *Status* as a loved and satisfied person. The *Way out* to normal freedom and selfhood. Courageous ethical motivation is felt here. Is prepared for outgoing relationships. Phase 4. The dynamic income is expended in 'work'. The *Achievement* of limited skills in relationships, in tolerance of frustration, in learning and in play.'[1]

If the mother fails in this task, and according to the degree of her failure, the disposition of the child will develop abnormal traits. Basically, security is what the infant needs, and security means reliability and regularity in the behaviour of the mother towards her child: in a word, this means the uniformity of law. The good mother is 'always the same'—not a person of unpredictable moods. The infant, however, must learn to pass on beyond this. If not, if it is 'tied to its mother's apron strings' and fails gradually to achieve independence and to stand on its own feet, again the result will be the development of abnormal and pathological traits. This 'launching out into the deep' requires courage; but if the mother has rightly played her part, the infant will find itself able to take this critical step with confidence and thus find its freedom. With one part of itself it will not want to be free; it will selfishly cling to its mother and 'fear to launch away'. But only by acquiring this independence and accepting responsibility can it find true happiness. The security, however, is not left behind; it is integrated in the freedom of living dangerously. As a modern psychiatrist has said, 'Safety first' is the ideal motto for road users but it is the worst possible motto for life.

From what has been said it is clear that the development of the infant is fraught with many and great psychological dangers. Both security and independence are required—a fact which unfortunately is not by any

---

[1] Frank Lake; *Clinical Theology* (1966), p. 140,

means always recognised. The tendency only too often is to go to one or other of the two extremes. If security is over-emphasised, you have legalism and ultra-authoritarianism. If freedom and independence is over-emphasised, you have rebellion and licence. In fact, both security and independence, both law and liberty must be held in tension together.

We see, therefore, that to make Christian morality a question of either or—either obedience to moral laws and principles or freedom and self-expression—is a fatal and false antithesis. That is precisely where the exponents of the new morality have gone wrong. True freedom can be achieved only by obedience to principles. Thus, for example, it is with the musical composer and the artist in any medium. He finds his freedom in obeying and surrendering to the principles of his art. He never feels so free as when he is doing this. But life is more than art. The latter is departmental and part of a greater whole; and the art of living is to find one to whom one can surrender one's *whole* personality, and that One is the Creator, God Himself. Only in Him can the individual lose his whole self; only in Him can he find his whole self, *cui servire regnare est.*

If we like, we can say that this submission is to the law and rule of love. As we saw in an earlier chapter, this means submission to God, the *Ens Realissimum*; for, according to Christian teaching, at least, God is Love. In other words, love is the stuff of which the universe is made, and love means self-oblation not self-assertion. But this picture and pattern of human conduct, if it is to avail as a guide to life, needs to be filled in with the details of moral virtues and moral laws and practical duties. Otherwise, in practice it is too vague and generalised to be an adequate guide at all. We shall return to this point shortly.

This brings us to our second question. How, in practice, is the individual to learn rightly to surrender himself so that he may attain the moral goal; how, in a word, is he to lose his life so that he may find it, as our Lord taught.

In trying to answer this question we must call to our aid the doctrine of the Holy Spirit—the Cinderella of theological studies. We have seen that the exponents of the new morality have rightly drawn attention to the fact that in assessing every moral situation we have to take into account not only the factors of which we are fully conscious, but also unconscious influences. Different schools of psychology estimate these differently. For Freud the unconscious is an 'it', or, to use his word, an *Id*—the repository of repressions. For Jung, on the other hand, it is something living and purposive—or, at least, it can be—leading the psyche on to fuller life. The Christian theologian here will find himself in agreement with Jung. The unconscious, for him, is the seat of the operations of the Holy Spirit in man—the fine point of the soul (*apex mentis*) at which God most profoundly influences and directs the life of man, leading each individual, who is receptive to his gracious influences, to fulfil his true vocation and destiny.[1]

This is not an entirely new point of view. It was at least dimly perceived by the ancients in their attitude to dreams as foreshadowing the future and issuing warnings —a doctrine now much more clearly understood, and accepted by psychologists, who all recognise the truth of Freud's dictum that dreams are the royal road to the unconscious. So we often find it in Holy Scripture. Joseph's dream that he and his brothers were harvesting and that their sheaves bowed down before his sheaf clearly foretold the manifestation of his powers of leadership—especially when supported by another similar

[1] See *The Holy Spirit and Modern Thought* (1959), p. 166, where I have worked this out more fully.

dream. This repetition of a theme we now know to be especially significant. Negative or warning dreams are also mentioned in the Bible. According to the Matthaean tradition Joseph was 'warned of God in a dream' not to return into Egypt, although unfortunately the actual dream is not recorded. Similarly S. Peter had a warning dream telling him to disregard his Jewish prejudices in his dealings with gentiles—a warning to which he gave heed, although later he went back on it. All this is thoroughly up to date, and can be matched many times by those of us who know how to interpret our own dreams. In this way, in addition to others, we know full well we can receive the Holy Spirit's guidance, our eyes being opened to see things which unconsciously we have been refusing to see.

Thus every believing Christian can be confident that he has within himself the guidance of God, the Holy Spirit, if only he can learn to be receptive to it. There are, indeed, a good many Christians in these days who have learned how to profit from this aspect of the Spirit's guidance. It is a pity that there are not more, for the technique of interpreting one's own dreams is quite simple. Unfortunately there is much prejudice to be overcome in this quarter, and there are still too many people who suppose that dreams are 'all nonsense'.

It sometimes happens, however, that there may appear to be a clash between the guidance received through the unconscious and moral laws and standards; and of course there are psychiatrists who in such circumstances will advise the 'patient' to set the latter at naught. But this is certainly not the case with all or even most psychiatrists; and, equally certainly, it is not required of any Christian moralist to say that all moral laws and rules must, therefore, be jettisoned, as the custom of some is. The matter is not as simple as that. Where a clash of the kind indicated does occur, experience shows that a quiet waiting upon God will, in the majority of cases, enable the individual gradually to arrive at a practical solution of his doubts without setting at naught any Christian or basic moral law or principle. But it may not turn out thus, and where that is the case the individual must follow the dictates of his own conscience. Those who attack moral theology often seem to forget that there is no more fundamental principle in it than the principle that the individual conscience must in the last resort always be obeyed: *Conscientia semper sequenda est.* This holds good however revolutionary the resulting action may be. There is no question of the individual conscience being crushed by authority, as sometimes seems to be suggested. Bishop Kirk truly said of this doctrine of the liberty of conscience that it is 'the proud possession of Christendom in all its branches—one of the unique gifts of Christ to the world'.[1]

In facing all questions of conscience, however, it is a great advantage if the individual is able to consult a wise counsellor; indeed it may be essential because everybody has the duty of seeing that his conscience is properly enlightened, and it is often not easy for the individual concerned to judge rightly in matters which concern him so closely. Here the counsellor, if he is wise, will act as a kind of midwife, assisting the 'patient' to discover what his own conscience is bringing forth.

It sometimes happens, and it should more often happen, that a person can obtain great help with his personal problems by becoming a member of a Christian group or cell in which he is able to share his doubts and difficulties with other Christians in what the New Testament calls the *Koinonia* of the Spirit. There are dangers here, of course. Membership of such a group may become a fettering rather than a liberating experience, if the group is inward-looking rather than outward-

---

[1] K. E. Kirk: *Conscience and its Problems* (1927), p. 61.

looking. But membership of a spiritually healthy and enlightened group can be a most valuable and educative experience.

Such, then, is the task of the moral theologian today. The prevailing moral confusion has rendered his task not less necessary but more, and, as time goes on, I believe that this will become increasingly apparent.

One more thing remains to be said, and, as I think, it is of the utmost importance; the more so since it is often totally ignored by many of those who write on moral questions in these days. It is—to use the words of Bishop Butler—that 'the least observation will show, how little the generality of men are capable of speculations. Therefore morality and religion must be somewhat plain and easy to be understood'.[1] We must never forget that the majority of the human race are plain and simple people. Even today two-fifths of mankind are unable to read or write; and, what is more, more than half of the people in the world are under twenty-one years of age. These people need detailed moral guidance. It is emphatically not enough to tell them: Love and do what you like. They will not resent moral guidance, if it is given in the right way. Everything depends on that.

If, for example, the Ten Commandments are put before them as a rigid authoritarian system of morals which they have to obey willy nilly, very many of them will repudiate them and kick over the traces. But if these are put before them rather as being a book of instructions for living issued by our Maker, comparable to the booklets issued by modern manufacturers of motor cars, T. V. sets and all the other modern appliances, they will see the sense of this, and at least will feel no resentment. Certainly a modern moralist who gives the impression that the Ten Commandments are entirely obsolete for a Christian today is doing a great disservice to mankind.

[1] Joseph Butler, Sermon 5, *On Compassion.*

The task of the moral theologian is not to jettison the Decalogue, but to explain it—as, in fact, Our Lord did— by showing that these Commandments must all be re-interpreted in terms of the Tenth, which is the only one directly concerned with our thoughts. To put it in another way, they must be observed not simply externally but internally. It is not enough to refrain from adultery; we must avoid harbouring adulterous thoughts. It is not enough to refrain from murder; we must not harbour thoughts of hatred against anybody, and so forth. It is not difficult for simple people to understand that it is reasonable to give heed to such directions which many centuries of human experience have endorsed as containing the best moral guidance available for human society. Nor is it really difficult to show that to give heed to these directions does not fetter our human freedom, but rather enhances it, just as obeying the book of instructions issued by the manufacturer enhances our freedom to drive our car. Of course, we are all free to ignore the Ten Commandments if we choose, just as we are free to ignore the instructions issued by the makers of our motor car or motor cycle; but if we do, we shall probably live to regret it, and, what is more, we shall not only suffer ourselves for our neglect but we may bring suffering upon others also. Despite all the changes which have come upon the modern world, the guidance of the moral theologian is still required, and, if it is offered with tact and common sense, in the majority of cases it will not be resented but welcomed.

Additional Note on the authority of Convocation

Until the setting up of the projected General Synod, the Convocations remain the ultimate canonical authority in the Church of England. This authority is expressed in Canons, Acts of Convocation and resolutions of Convocation. An Act of Convocation is a Resolution passed in identical terms by both Houses and declared by the President to be an Act of Convocation. Thus Gibson says: 'All synodical acts, to which the royal licence is not necessary, receive their final authority from the sanction of the metropolitan.'[1] An Act of Convocation has exactly the same spiritual authority as a Canon. The sole difference between the two is that, owing to the provisions of the iniquitous Act of the Submission of the Clergy (1534), the Convocations cannot pass canons without the sanction of the Crown. This means that they are enforceable in law, whereas Acts of Convocation are not. There is no substance in the opinion sometimes expressed that 'An Act of Convocation has the authority only of a strong expression of opinion or at most a recommendation, and not the binding force of a Canon', to quote a recent writer[2] who argues that the marriage regulations at present operative in the Church of England, which derive their authority from Acts of Convocation, and not from Canons, cannot therefore be regarded as strictly binding.

This view is entirely mistaken. Thus, when the Convocation of Canterbury recently reaffirmed the principle of the seal of confession in April 1959, the President, in declaring this to be an Act of Convocation, said: 'What we are doing is reaffirming the principle of the seal of confession, which has been in the canons all along, *with the fullest possible power that Convocation possesses*'[3] (italics mine).

[1] E. Gibson: *Synodus Anglicana*, Chap. 16, section 183.
[2] A. R. Winnett: *The Church and Divorce* (1968), p. 102.
[3] *Chronicle of the Convocation of Canterbury*, April 1959, p. 231.

215

Index

Aberfan disaster, 132
Abortion, 84ff., 193, 195
Absolution, 143ff.
Agape, 10, 18
Aristotle, 28, 70, 72
Articles, Thirty-Nine, 103f.
Artificial Insemination, 87ff.
Augustine, 9n., 25, 95, 104, 117,
  148ff., 161f., 178
Barry, Bishop F. R., 83, 106
Bell, Bishop George, 184
Blackstone, 95
Boe, E. E., 22
Butler, Bishop, 13n., 43, 134, 204n.,
  213

Canon Law Commission, 175
Canon Law, History of, 177ff.
Canons of 1603, 179f.
Casuistry, Chap. 4 *passim*
Chesterton, G. K., 205
Church and State, 169ff.
Circumstances of an action, 36ff.
Clinical theology, 12ff., 17ff.
Confession, seal of, 16, 174
Conscience, erring 54ff.
  doubtful, 62ff.
  scrupulous, 58ff.
Consequences of an action, 39ff.
Contraception, vi, 74ff., 189ff., 194f.

Dante, 152
Darwin, 199
Death of God theology, 205
Determinism, 22
Double Effect, principle of, 40f., 73,
  85, 96

Drug addiction, 126f.

Ecclesiastical Jurisdiction Measure,
  176f., 183ff.
Euthanasia, 92ff.

Fénelon, 2, 153
Figgis, J. N., 170
Fletcher, J., 90, 202
Forgiveness, 139ff.
Freedom, 21
Freud, S., 14f., 19, 46, 49ff., 109,
  198, 200ff., 210

Gambling, 97ff.
Garbett, Archbishop, 182, 184
Graham, Billy, 171
Grotius, 104f.
Group psychotherapy, 18

Häring, B., 43
Henderson and Gillespie, 59f.
Henson, Bishop, 147
Hermas, 142
Homicide Act (1957), 27
Hooker, R., 8, 144ff., 179
Humility, 163f.
Hypnosis, 25

Ignorance, vincible and invincible,
  55f.
Illingworth, J. R., 153
Imitatio Christi, 147
Inge, Dean, 118
Intention, 33ff.

217

Johnson, Dr., 24
Jones, Ernest, 53
Jung, C. G., 210

Kirk, Bishop, 29f., 56, 115, 119, 122,
    142f., 173, 197, 212
Koinonia of the Spirit, 13, 20, 212

Lake, F., 12, 113, 207f.
Lambeth Conferences, 186ff.
Lang, Archbishop, 175
Law, canon, 11
    human, 8f.
Lecky, W. E. H., 164ff.
Libertarianism, 22
Lindsay, A. D., 199f.
Love, 9, 11, 130f., 148ff.
    and moral rules, 162f.
    and the relation between societies,
        168f.

McDougall, W., 23
Mackenzie, J. S., 133f.
McNaghten Rules, 28
Marriage, nature of, 188ff., 196f.
Marx, Karl, 199ff.
Matthews, W. R., 89, 92
Methodists, 20
Moberly, R. C., 115, 139f.
Motive, 23, 32f.
Mottram, V. H., 27
Murray, Gilbert, 110

Newman, J. H., 118
Nietzsche, 205

Organ transplantation, 40

Paraklete, 17
Pascal, 65
Pavlov, 113
Pierce, C. A., 43
Premium Bonds, 102ff.
Probabiliorism, 71f.
Probabilism, 68ff., 78
Prümmer, M., 100f., 122

Punishment, Chap. 6 *passim*
    capital, 134ff.

Repentance, 3
Rigorism, 65ff.
Ritual prosecutions, 175, 182f.

Sanderson, Bishop, 2f., 30, 33, 44ff.,
    68f., 122
Sexual intercourse outside marriage,
    156ff., 193
Sin, mortal and venial, 5f., 116ff.
    actual and original, 111ff.
    actual and habitual, 114ff.
    formal and material, 121ff.
    occasions of, 125f.
Situational ethics, 202
Skinner, J., 1, 2, 16
Society of Friends, 20
Spinoza, 127
Sterilisation, 79ff., 195
Stock Exchange, 99
Suicide, 95ff.

Tawney, R. H., 166
Taylor, A. E., 109
Taylor, Bishop Jeremy, 9, 11, 31ff.,
    44, 54f., 68f., 105, 117f., 120,
    122, 124
Temple, Archbishop William, 11,
    109, 131f., 138ff., 167, 169, 175
Ten Commandments, 213f.
Tennant, F. R., 114
Tertullian, 142
Thomas Aquinas, 5, 8f., 29f., 79, 95,
    104, 136, 178

Vatican Council II, 75
Vietnam war, 107

Waddams, H., 9f.
War, 103ff.
    nuclear, 105ff.
Williams, Glanville, 91
Williams, H. A., 202ff.
Williams, Watkin, 121
Wood, T., 102